Why Do Governments Divest?

Springer
Berlin
Heidelberg
New York
Barcelona
Hong Kong
London
Milan
Paris
Singapore
Tokyo

Alfred Schipke

Why Do Governments Divest?

The Macroeconomics of Privatization

With 11 Figures
and 14 Tables

 Springer

Alfred Schipke
Harvard University
John F. Kennedy School of Government
Cambridge, MA 02138
United States
alfred_schipke@harvard.edu

ISBN 3-540-41579-3 Springer-Verlag Berlin Heidelberg New York

Library of Congress Cataloging-in-Publication Data
Die Deutsche Bibliothek – CIP-Einheitsaufnahme
Schipke, Alfred: Why do governments divest?: with 14 tables / Alfred Schipke. – Berlin; Heidelberg;
New York; Barcelona; Hong Kong; London; Milan; Paris; Singapore; Tokyo: Springer, 2001
    ISBN 3-540-41579-3

Springer-Verlag Berlin Heidelberg New York
a member of BertelsmannSpringer Science+Business Media GmbH

© Springer-Verlag Berlin · Heidelberg 2001
Printed in Germany

Hardcover-Design: Erich Kirchner, Heidelberg

SPIN 10547583   42/2202-5 4 3 2 1 0 – Printed on acid-free paper

Preface

A review of the past 40 years reveals that economic policymaking has been profoundly influenced by two major phenomena. In the 1960s and 1970s, the Keynesian "revolution" made its debut on the stage of economic policy and determined the actions of policymakers in the Western world. The last two decades of the past millennium in turn were influenced by the phenomenon of privatization. While the application of Keynesian ideas to economic policymaking was based on fundamentally new insights into the workings of national economies, privatization lacks such new insights but instead reverts back to "old" and largely neoclassical principles. However, despite the lack of a new theoretical framework, the policy implications and the scope of the current privatization wave exceed even that of the Keynesian revolution, since it is not limited to western countries alone but is on the policy agenda of practically every government in the world.

I was first exposed to policy issues of privatization in 1990, when I had the opportunity to work with Jeffrey Sachs in Poland during the country's first year of economic transformation and liberalization. Since then I have been involved with various issues of privatization in a number of countries and taught several courses on the subject. My continued interest in the subject is related to the fact that it can be analyzed from many different vantage points, given that privatization is by its very nature an interdisciplinary topic. It appears—as in so many other areas of economic policy—that political considerations rather than economics are the main driving force. Despite the countless publications that exist on the subject, many aspects of privatization have still been neglected or only recently received some attention. This book tries to fill part of the gap by introducing the reader to macroeconomic aspects of privatization and how these are related to the political economy of policymaking.

As with any major project, the writing of this book was directly related to the support of others. I was particularly fortunate in having had a great mentor and advisor. Dieter Cassel at Gerhard-Mercator University not only first introduced me to the field of macroeconomics and inspired me to be interested in issues of economic policy, but has been a dedicated supporter throughout. At the International Monetary Fund, I am particularly thankful to Luis Eduardo Escobar.

My collaboration with him on Jamaica did not only sharpen my understanding of the many economic and political facets of the country, but also resulted in a friendship. I especially appreciate his very insightful comments on the Jamaican case study. I have also profited from Audrey Watson who revealed yet another talent, namely that of being a great editor. I am very thankful for her many comments and willingness to review the manuscript.

Cambridge, Massachusetts
November 2000

1 Introduction

Over the past two decades, the world has experienced privatization on a massive scale. Industrial and developing countries alike are putting up entire sectors for sale, including those once considered off limits, such as telecommunications, railroads, and national airlines. The numbers speak for themselves. According to Privatization International, more than 100 countries have divested public assets. In 1997, the value of worldwide privatization reached a record sum of more than U.S.$162 billion, equivalent to 0.5 percent of world economic output. The three preceding years had already seen record levels of privatization of U.S.$90 billion, U.S.$76 billion and U.S.$78 billion respectively.[1] In addition to western Europe, Latin America, and Asia, numerous African countries have lately joined the movement, as have countries that are still under communist rule, such as China and Cuba.[2]

This privatization movement also encompassed the formerly socialist economies, where the demise of socialism was accompanied by a drastic reduction in public ownership. Prior to the economic transformation in central and eastern Europe, the number of state-owned enterprises in these countries was estimated at almost 90,000, of which 25,000 were thought to be in Russia alone. If the formerly public enterprises of eastern Germany are added, the total number of public enterprises increases to over 100,000, of which more than 40 percent have been sold or liquidated.[3] While these numbers should be viewed with skepticism, since they certainly do not reveal the quality of privatization and the extent to which the new owners have now secured property rights, they are indicative of the massive transfer of ownership that has taken place and they suggest that privatization will remain an issue for quite some time to come.[4]

---

[1] See Baker (1998).

[2] See Gibbon (1997).

[3] See OECD (1994).

[4] Young and Reynolds (1994) argue that the quality of privatization in post-communist countries is very poor, and that unless additional institutional changes are made, "what will result will not be real market economies, but inefficient, partially collectivized, hybrid

Why have policymakers across the globe suddenly embraced privatization? One could argue that they learned from their past mistakes: in order to improve living standards and welfare, policymakers abandoned poor economic policies based on government intervention and public ownership and instead began to embrace market-driven economies based on private ownership. Certainly, economic constraints forced policymakers to search for new alternatives. In the case of former socialist countries, the prevalent economic model based on public ownership and central planning had gone bankrupt. In the case of developing countries, the poor economic growth performance and high rates of inflation and in some countries even outright hyperinflation in the 1970s and 1980s had undermined the then-popular view that economic development could be achieved only through government-led growth and import substitution. Even industrialized countries were faced with the sustainability of their generous and growing welfare states and the limits on taxation of their citizens. The frequent call for "fiscal consolidation"[5] in these countries has often been synonymous with a call for less government involvement and less public ownership.[6]

While these developments contributed to an apparent reversal of policies in many countries, it would be incautious to assume that policymakers suddenly embraced privatization solely to improve the welfare of their populations. Caution is warranted for at least two reasons. On the one hand, it can be observed that the current wave of privatization is nearly universal, although varying in degree, irrespective of a country's level of economic development, system of political governance, political parties and ideologies. However, it does not seem likely that policymakers across countries and systems are subscribing to the same, largely neoclassical, economic model. On the other hand, governments in the past have all too often pursued economic policies that were clearly at odds with the maximization of economic welfare. Instead, their own political goals often led them to favor policies that, from the outset, were unsustainable in the long run. It seems unlikely that the objective functions of politicians and policymakers have suddenly changed.[7]

However, even if politicians and policymakers continue to pursue the same objectives, it is true that the current wave of privatization was preceded by a change in paradigm that now allows policymakers to use the sale of assets as an additional tool of public policy. This is in sharp contrast to the paradigm that prevailed only two decades ago, when large-scale privatization would have been inconceivable in most parts of the world, including in industrialized countries. It appears that the

---

economies in which a bureaucratic elite still succeeds in exploiting the bulk of the population."

[5] In Germany, the term "Haushaltskonsolidierung" (budget consolidation) was even voted most popular word of the year in 1995.

[6] See World Bank (1997).

[7] Alesina and Drazen (1991), for example, explain the delay of economic stabilization on the basis of a "war of attrition" model.

change in paradigm was brought about by a number of fairly unrelated and coincidental factors and cannot be explained on the basis of a single event. It is, for example, quite surprising that the paradigm shift can be traced back to the first large-scale privatization in the U.K. Economic conditions in the U.K. were clearly less adverse than those in many other countries, including the former socialist economies and many developing countries, where real constraints warranted a dramatic shift in economic policies, including a reduction of the public sector. In terms of the role and size of the public sector relative to the overall size of the economy, the U.K. trailed even such countries as France, Spain, and Sweden. These comparisons suggest that privatization in Britain was initiated more on political than on economic grounds.

While the change in paradigm cannot be traced to a single event, policymakers now have an additional policy tool to further their objectives, including those that conflict with the promotion of economic efficiency and growth. In particular, governments might sell individual assets at a discount to loyal and influential constituencies and key voter groups, increasing the wealth and income of these interest groups without due consideration for improving efficiency. Such motives have been attributed not only to developing countries and transition economies but even to large industrialized countries such as Great Britain during its initial privatization program. Heald, for example, points out that:

the rationale for the [privatization] programme was invented after the event. In particular, economists have attempted to adopt and redirect the programme, highlighting the efficiency rationale, with limited, but variable, success. Much of the telling criticism has (at least implicitly) come from a market-oriented perspective, namely that the government was not taking its own efficiency objectives seriously enough (Heald 1989, 43).

For quite some time, the United Kingdom engaged in privatization methods that were considered contrary to the goal of economic efficiency. Shares were sold under market value and rationed, effectively leading to a targeted transfer of government wealth and income to particular groups in society.[8] It is not surprising that polls taken after the first companies had been sold at a discount to citizens showed that 57 percent of the people who bought shares in one of the privatized companies—including factory laborers, the hard core of Labour's historic base—planned to vote Conservative in the June 1987 election. Exit polls in that election showed that 6 out of 10 people who owned shares voted Tory.[9] The political rationale behind such a policy is, of course, that lucky investors enjoying windfall profits as a result of the intentional under-valuation are aware of their gain, whereas taxpayers—the losers in this transfer game—are more likely to be indifferent because of their marginal stake.[10] It appears that the ability of policymakers to transfer wealth and income as a result of the paradigm change helps explain the general popularity of privatization.

---

[8] This method was dubbed "people's capitalism".

[9] See Harvard Business School (1988).

[10] See Schipke (1994).

Given the large size of some of the divestment programs, the sale of assets might produce not only a direct transfer of wealth but also macroeconomic consequences. This in turn implies that policymakers can use privatization not only to direct resources to particular groups in society but also to influence short-term macroeconomic aggregates in a pre-determined direction. The use of privatization for short-term macroeconomic reasons is likely to be motivated by the probability of getting re-elected in the case of an incumbent party or by rewarding political followers with preferred macroeconomic outcomes such as low rates of inflation, increases in output, or low rates of unemployment. Of course, the necessary requirement for such an assumption is that the country has a sufficiently large stock of public assets to produce macroeconomic impacts through privatization. Analogous to the "direct buyout" of selected groups of voters through the redistribution of government assets, politicians could use privatization to increase their popularity—or at least limit any loss of popularity—in the short run, without due regard for long-run considerations. While the use of privatization for short-term macroeconomic objectives will be temporary, the relatively large stock of public assets in many countries would allow governments to continue using privatization for this purpose over a number of years.

Clearly, there is a substantial downside to policies that are driven by macroeconomic objectives other than fostering growth and improving living standards in the long term. For example, policymakers could rely on privatization to alleviate the impact of internal or external macroeconomic disequilibria instead of implementing politically costly "real" adjustment measures that address the underlying causes of fiscal and balance-of-payments deficits. Under such circumstances governments might, for example, be inclined to grant monopoly rights to utilities in order to maximize sales receipts. Furthermore, governments might embark on large-scale privatization programs to influence macroeconomic variables in the short term instead of using the divestment effort to improve the structure of the economy and hence long-term output growth.

The advent of privatization as a widely used tool of public policy can be seen as similar to the general acceptance of Keynesian economics decades earlier. Buchanan and Wagner (1977) argue that the paradigm shift that led to the general acceptance of Keynesianism gave politicians the opportunity to use stabilization policies to foster their own agendas and to please voters. For example, governments were able to increase public spending for political reasons without having to rely on raising politically costly taxes—and all of this was done, of course, in the name of economic stabilization. Today, a similar argument could be made about privatization, since policymakers can—at least while there is a substantial stock of public assets—use privatization to please voters, this time all in the name of economic efficiency. And analogous to the case of Keynesian deficit spending, voters might be unable to judge whether politicians are engaging in privatization to maximize social welfare or to foster their own cause at the expense of overall economic well-being. Under those circumstances, and comparable to the widespread misuse of aggregate demand management in the 1960s and 1970s, privatization is likely not to generate the expected improvements in economic growth and the living standard. Indeed, increased economic growth and improved efficiency are, at best, side products, the population could call for more government intervention, leading to a new wave of nationalizations and the re-acquisition of formerly privatized assets. The pendulum of public versus private ownership would once again swing in the opposite direction.[11]

This study will focus primarily on evidence from industrialized and developing countries to support the hypothesis that governments have incentives to employ privatization for macroeconomic-related political reasons. However, the question arises as to whether the hypothesis also holds for former socialist economies in transition. One common feature of transition economies is mass privatization, which is often synonymous with giving public shares to private citizens free of charge (directly or through the issue of vouchers) or at a nominal fee that is substantially less than the net present value of the assets. Of course, pursuing such an approach is not likely to allow policymakers to exploit privatization for short-term macroeconomic reasons.[12] Therefore, it is unlikely that macroeconomic goals enter the objective function of politicians during the initial transition period. Instead, during this period, privatization is used as a means of securing the political transition from centralized bureaucracies to more decentralized democracies. Giving shares to private groups will in turn raise their stake in the new system and will make them ultimate defenders of that system. However, once a certain degree of political stability has been reached, macroeconomic stabilization assumes a more prominent role and the objective function changes. During this second stage, policymakers in transition economies may behave like those in developing and industrialized countries. This seems to be confirmed by developments in the states of the former Soviet Union. Countries that have reached the greatest degree of political stability, for example the Baltic States, have moved toward focusing on macroeconomic stabilization and might hence have an incentive to use privatization for such a purpose.

Despite the potential macroeconomic implications and the incentive for policymakers to use privatization for such an end, most research on privatization has focused either on microeconomic aspects or on operational issues such as the choice of privatization methods and techniques of valuation.[13] This study will focus instead on macroeconomic aspects of privatization, examining in a comprehensive manner the effects of privatization on key macroeconomic factors such as growth, monetary and fiscal outcomes, balance of payments, and employment issues. In addition, it will analyze the potential use of privatization to accomplish broader

---

[11] On the question of whether there are cycles of privatization and nationalization, see Siegmund (1996).

[12] The exception is that mass privatization can be used to limit the inflationary impact of a monetary overhang that might have existed prior to the transformation period.

[13] A few studies have started to focus on aspects such as fiscal and monetary issues of privatization. See, for example, Davies, et. al. (2000). For an overview of traditional microeconomic aspects of privatization see, for example, Bös (1991), Maskin (1992) and Galal, et. al. (1992). On privatization methods see Vuylstek (1989).

policy objectives that might not necessarily coincide with increases in efficiency and growth. Chapter 2 reviews the theoretical and empirical literature of private versus public ownership as it relates to efficiency and growth, including the recent discussion of privatizing pay-as-you-go social security systems.

Chapter 3 assesses whether policymakers have an incentive to engage in privatization for short-term political reasons that are potentially inconsistent with the growth and efficiency objectives most often mentioned in the context of privatization. Theories of politics in macroeconomic policymaking have attempted to explain why governments often delay macroeconomic reforms even in light of greater adjustment costs in the future and why governments try to manipulate macroeconomic aggregates to boost their popularity or to please particular constituencies. Since it is argued that policymakers might use privatization to affect macroeconomic outcomes for political reasons, these theories provide some guidance for the subsequent analysis.

Chapter 4 attempts to show that fiscal considerations are often a prime motive for governments to engage in privatization. It is argued that from a fiscal point of view, governments should divest only if this leads to an improvement in the intertemporal budget constraint. However, it is shown that policymakers are instead inclined to divest public assets as a means of loosening the one-period budget constraint as well as for political reasons. This chapter also includes a case study on the sale of assets in Germany in the context of European Monetary Union, showing that even industrialized countries with developed capital markets might resort to privatization for fiscal reasons.

Besides fiscal considerations, large privatization programs have potential implications for inflation, employment, and the balance of payments. These issues are covered in more depth in Chapter 5. Furthermore, a case study on Pakistan is used to illustrate the tendency of policymakers to limit adverse employment effects of privatization by resorting to massive transfer payments that can negatively affect the macroeconomy, undermining the very rationale for privatization.

In Chapter 6, a simple framework is used to analyze the potential macroeconomic implications of privatization in a consistent manner. Since this model is similar to the framework of a financial program used by many governments to simulate and operationalize macroeconomic policy objectives, it serves to demonstrate in a quantitative manner why governments might pursue particular privatization strategies.

Given that many countries started their large-scale privatization programs only a few years ago, while others are currently in the midst of their divestment efforts, the evidence of privatization failures is still scant and a reversal of the current privatization wave seems remote. However, the first country has already come full circle and de-facto re-nationalized many of the entities that had been transferred to the private sector. As the case study on Jamaica in Chapter 7 demonstrates, the causes are closely linked to the politically motivated macroeconomic reasons for divesting the public assets in the first place. Despite the fact that the country is still an isolated case, it serves as prime example of how ill-perceived privatization programs can create a backlash. This example is especially telling, since Jamaica's privatization and liberalization effort was once considered a model in the late 1980s by both the Reagan and Thatcher administrations. Chapter 8 concludes the study.

2 Economic Growth and Efficiency

The decision to reduce the economic role of the government through privatization should be guided primarily by whether this will lead to an improvement in the economy's growth potential. The current global enthusiasm for privatization suggests that most governments have concluded that this is indeed the case and that a reduction in government activity will be synonymous with improvements in economic efficiency and growth. Such a view is quite contrary to the one that prevailed only a couple of decades earlier. While today the political and academic discussion centers around the inefficiency of governments in general and public enterprises in particular, in the past the focus was on market failures and the consequent need for governments to participate actively in the marketplace, including in the production of goods and services.

Although a general distrust of the private sector existed in most industrialized countries, the call for government involvement was especially pronounced in developing countries that were attempting to catch up with the more advanced economies. It was seen as imperative that the government assume a leading role in improving living standards. In combination with the import-substitution policy, with its emphasis on the protection of infant industries through high tariffs, the development of an industrial sector was also encouraged through a system of indirect incentives as well as outright public ownership of productive enterprises.[14] In addition, the literature on economic development pointed out that the private sector's failure to generate adequate savings and investment undermined the growth potential of such economies. Gillis, et. al., for example, state that:

One of the basic tenets of typical development strategies of the 1950s and 1960s was that investment expansion required for sustained income growth could not proceed in the absence of major efforts to increase the share of government savings in GDP. It was commonly held that growth in private savings was inherently constrained by such factors as low per-capita incomes and high private consumption propensities among wealthy families with the greatest capacity for savings (Gillis, et. al. 1983, 273).

---

[14] On the original arguments for an import substitution policy see Prébisch (1950). Bruton (1989) provides a summary of theories that are related to the import substitution strategy.

The obvious policy conclusion was to increase the tax ratio and to use the resources to finance infrastructure projects and to establish public enterprises, especially in the manufacturing sector. However, many of the investment projects had low marginal products of capital and in order to sustain high growth rates over time more and more public resources were needed, eventually increasing fiscal deficits and raising inflation rates.[15] Furthermore, it turned out that governments often expanded consumption spending rather than public investment.

A similar rationale was inherent in the industrialization models of the former socialist countries, where an omnipotent government sector was seen as necessary to catch up with Western industrialized countries. These economies relied on a growth strategy based on "forced" savings and investment. With investment shares of, for example, up to 30 percent in the case of the Soviet Union, aggregate output initially increased by about 5 percent per annum during the period 1950 to 1979. The growth performance in other socialist countries was quite similar. However, as in the case of developing countries, it turned out that the marginal product of capital ultimately diminished and changes in total factor productivity contributed little to output growth. Hence, high growth rates were sustainable only through ever-increasing investment and at the expense of consumption.[16] As Kornai puts it:

in the language of growth theory, they have dangling before them (even if they never heard of one) a Harrod-Domar model with just a single factor of production: capital. To their extremely simplified reasoning, the larger the proportion for investment, the faster the rate of growth (Kornai 1992, 167).

However, as Scully points out:

the effect of an increase in the growth rate of the capital-labor ratio on the growth rate of GDP per capita ultimately depends on how efficiently the resources are employed in the economy. For equal rates of capital formation, economies that transform inputs into output relatively inefficiently will grow more slowly than efficient economies (Scully 1988, 655).

While there is little disagreement that the past growth strategies of both developing countries and socialist economies, with their heavy reliance on the government as the key engine of economic growth, were bound to fail, the same does not necessarily apply to the so-called East Asian development model—at least prior to the 1997-98 financial crises. Given their stellar growth performance, with average annual growth rates of output per person in excess of 6 percent over a thirty-year period, the evidence seemed to suggest that the "right" kind of government intervention, focusing on investment and an outward-oriented strategy, is conducive to economic development.[17] Although direct ownership of non-financial enterprises by the public sector was less pronounced than, for example, in Latin America, the government exercised substantial control over private entities by directing credits to

---

[15] The large public sector fiscal deficits in the 1970s and early 1980s were to a large extent caused by the performance of the public sector in general and public enterprises in particular, which frequently engaged in operating practices that were not cost-minimizing and set prices below marginal costs. See also the chapter on fiscal considerations of privatization.

[16] For an international comparison of investment shares and growth rates see Kornai (1992).

[17] On growth in the East Asian economies see also Crafts (1998) and Sarel (1995).

selected conglomerates and owning key financial intermediaries.[18] Even prior to the East Asian financial crisis, a number of studies showed that the Asian miracle was not much of a miracle at all, but the result of a massive effort to mobilize resources for investment. For example, Young (1994) shows that the high growth rates of South Korea, Singapore, and Taiwan were largely the result of high rates of investment rather than improvements in total factor productivity. Krugman (1994) even compares the growth strategy of the Asian Tigers to that of the Soviet Union in the 1950s. Although unlike in the Soviet Union, a substantial portion of savings were generated by the private sector, the government sector also contributed substantially to savings: the public sector savings rates amounted on average to 3.8 percent, 15.7 percent, and 6.8 percent of GDP in South Korea, Singapore, and Taiwan respectively during the period 1985-91.[19] The East Asian financial crisis, however, has brought to the fore that while the reliance on government involvement can be quite successful initially, for example, in mobilizing and directing resources, the lack of a market-based allocation of resources ultimately risks channeling investments to wasteful projects with low returns or leading to outright crony capitalism. In other words, a reduction of government intervention and the privatization of productive enterprises and financial entities in the East Asian countries will be necessary to ensure that resources are allocated efficiently.

2.1   Growth theories and empirical growth studies

The extent to which a reduction in government economic activity has implications for output growth depends on whether and to what degree privatization affects the national savings rate, the level of capital investment (both physical and human), the efficiency with which available resources are used, and the rate of technological progress. Furthermore, whether the divestment of public enterprises has a one-time or transitory impact or instead affects economic growth permanently depends on which model captures growth processes most adequately.

In the context of neoclassical growth models like those of Swan (1956) and Solow (1956), privatization is likely to have a one-time impact on output if the transfer to the private sector is associated with a more efficient use of given resources (see section 2.2). While the improvements in efficiency are not necessarily related to who owns the productive assets, it is generally assumed that companies owned by the private sector are more likely to behave as profit maximizers and therefore have an incentive to minimize costs and employ inputs in the most efficient manner. Furthermore, the principal-agent literature points out that large organizations are prone to inefficiencies due to the separation of ownership and control.[20] Given that

---

[18] The apparent success of the East Asia development model caused the World Bank in 1991 to announce a major initiative to study the relationship between public policy in these countries and economic development. See World Bank (1993).

[19] See Sachs and Warner (1996).

[20] See Arrow (1985).

owners, managers, and workers of large companies and bureaucracies are likely to have different objective functions and that the monitoring of employees is costly, employees can shirk, which in turn is likely to lead to a suboptimal allocation of resources. While both public and private organizations are prone to such inefficiencies, the existence of a market for corporate control and the potential threat of takeovers assures that the interests of private owners and employees are aligned. Hence, privatizations that result in the issue of publicly traded stocks are likely to lead to improvements in x-efficiency.[21]

Another argument that is frequently put forward is related to the fact that large-scale privatization can potentially reduce government deficits and thereby contribute to increases in national savings and investment (see section 4). In the context of the Swan-Solow model, a privatization-related increase in savings and investment would be associated with a higher growth rate until a new steady state level of capital is reached. Because of the assumption of diminishing marginal products, a privatization-related increase in savings and investment would, however, not permanently increase the growth rate. However, as long as the marginal product of capital is higher than the depreciation rate, the increase in the steady state capital level would ensure an improvement in economic well-being, since the economy would be moving closer to the Golden Rule level of higher consumption per capita.

While most of the immediate implications of privatization would result in temporary or one-time effects, if a privately operated company, liberated from pursuing political objectives and free to reduce red tape and bureaucracy, were to pursue and to adopt new technologies more aggressively and allow the development of a culture of entrepreneurship, one would expect privatization to go hand-in-hand with faster technological change. Under the Swan-Solow model, this improvement in the growth rate of technological progress would be consistent with a sustained increase in the growth rate of output, allowing per capita consumption to continue to increase even once the steady state is reached. If economic growth is, however, more adequately described by endogenous growth models, potential increases in savings and investment as a result of privatization might not only lead to temporary increases in economic growth but might even have sustainable impacts on the growth rate in the long run.[22] This would, for example, be the case if economic

---

[21] Leibenstein (1966) discusses the difference between x- and allocative efficiency. On privatization and efficiency see also Hartwig (1998).

[22] Growth models that explicitly include the government in the production function are designed to determine the optimal size of the government, although the focus is not on public enterprises. The impact of government on growth is due to the existence of externalities. Such externalities imply that an increase in government activity increases the marginal product of capital and therefore output per capita. However, since government activities ultimately have to be financed through taxes, an increase in such an activity is associated with a negative effect on the after-tax marginal product of capital. This implies that once a government has passed its optimal point, a reduction in government activity combined with a reduction in taxes would lead to a permanently higher growth rate. Besides the theoretical attractiveness of determining the optimal size of government in such a model, it is of little use for practitioners since it would be difficult to operationalize.

output could be described by a production function with constant marginal products, such as in the AK model, instead of a Cobb-Douglas function with diminishing marginal products.[23]

Irrespective of the assumption about the underlying growth model, privatization is more likely to have a large positive impact if resources are used more efficiently, the private sector is more dynamic and adopts new technologies more quickly than its public counterpart, and if privatization is associated with higher savings and investment. Given that public enterprises are controlled by the government and foreign ownership has traditionally been limited—although some countries in the past allowed joint ventures and countries such as China continue to experiment with some, albeit limited, forms of foreign participation--divestment might especially profit from the attraction of foreign direct investments (FDI). Privatization-related FDI are likely to contribute both to an acceleration of capital accumulation and a transfer of technology and managerial know-how.[24]

The implications of privatization for economic efficiency and growth, however, will to a large degree depend on the accompanying economic reforms rather than the mere reduction in government activity and the divestment of public assets. Reforms that affect the degree of competition, such as trade liberalization, the establishment of an adequate anti-trust policy, and the enforcement of hard budget constraints once companies operate in the private sector, will be especially influential in determining economic outcomes.

An empirical analysis of what determines growth is confronted with the problem that the theoretical growth literature gives little guidance as to what the true explanatory variables should be in a regression analysis. As indicated above, a privatization-induced increase in savings and investment or an improvement in technology are likely to lead to an improvement in the standard of living irrespective of the underlying growth model. However, the growth literature gives few answers as to what determines the level of, for example, technology, and hence empirical studies have relied to a large degree on trial and error. While cross-sectional growth studies do not explicitly account for public enterprises, they frequently include right-hand side variables that stand for the degree of private property in the country or the overall size of the government.

A natural starting point for such an analysis is to determine empirically whether private ownership in general can explain differences in economic growth across countries. Most of the recent empirical studies on growth include a number of institutional variables, including private property, in their growth equations. These studies seem to provide some evidence that the growth performance in countries with a higher proportion of private ownership is superior to that in countries with a large public sector. Scully, for example, looks at a broad range of institutional

---

[23] Gylfason (1998), for example, uses a production function with constant returns to scale to demonstrate the potential implications of privatization for economic growth. For an overview of the endogenous growth literature see Barro and Sala-i-Martin (1995)

[24] On foreign direct investment and privatization see Welfens (1994) and Welfens (1996).

variables in 115 countries, including private ownership, and comes to the conclusion that:

The institutional framework has significant and large effects on the efficiency and growth rates of economies. Politically open societies, which subscribe to the rule of law, to private property, and to the market allocation of resources, grow at three times the rate and are two and one-half times as efficient as societies in which these freedoms are abridged (Scully 1988, 655).

Private ownership seems to correlate positively with productivity. Such a positive relationship has been shown to hold even in the case of China. Xiao's (1991) analysis of total factor productivity across Chinese provinces strikingly reveals that provinces with a higher share of privately produced industrial output are likely to have higher total factor productivity. Such an approach runs the risk, however, of model mis-specification through omitted variables. Two studies have tried to address these shortcomings by including combinations of variables that have been found significant in existing growth studies. Levine and Renelt (1992) use Leamer's (1983, 1985) extreme bounds test to identify the robustness of the respective variables. However, due to the restrictiveness of the extreme bounds method, almost no variable is statistically significant. Sala-i-Martin (1997) also relies on the data of empirical growth studies and includes 63 variables that have been found statistically significant in at least one regression, but instead of relying on the extreme bounds test that classifies variables simply as "robust" or "non-robust," he looks at the entire distribution of the estimators of the variable of interest. To keep the number of possible combinations of variables manageable, he specifies models in which the growth vector (average growth rates between 1960 and 1992) is determined by a vector of the variable of interest; a vector of fixed variables that are frequently included in growth equations, that is, the initial level of growth, the life expectancy in 1960, the primary school enrollment rate in 1960; the average investment rate; and a vector of three variables that are taken from the remaining pool.[25]

The variables of Sala-i-Martin's study that capture the role of government in economic growth are the size of government consumption and investment as well as a variable that captures the organizational form of production. With respect to the last, Sala-i-Martin uses data from Hall and Jones (1996) based on a classification made by Freedom House (1994) which gives countries values ranging from zero to five depending on whether goods and services are produced by state-owned enterprises or the private sector. The more dominant the private sector is, the higher is the assigned value. Such a variable would be the closest proxy for whether there is empirical evidence that private sector production is more conducive to economic growth than its state-owned counterpart. The empirical evidence seems to suggest that the variable is strongly correlated with economic growth irrespective of whether or not the average investment rate is included in the growth regressions. Furthermore, the study seems to suggest that public spending does not significantly

---

[25] He initially runs all the models without the average investment rate. When the variable is excluded no distinction can be made whether the effects of the right-hand side variables on growth are due to an improvement in efficiency or because of the impact on investment.

affect growth. To the contrary, in the regressions that include the average investment rate, the share of public investment is significantly negatively correlated with growth. This, of course, suggests that holding total investment constant, private sector investment is more efficient than its public counterpart.

2.2   The impact of privatization on output

Given that at least immediately after privatization, the greatest gains in terms of output are achieved as a result of a reallocation of resources, the following uses an Edgeworth Box diagram and the production possibility frontier (PPF)   to demonstrate the implications of privatization-related increases in efficiency for the economy at large (see Figure 2.1). This simple economy consists of two firms where one firm produces good X and the other produces good Y. The inputs capital (K) and labor (L) are given and constant so that $K_x + K_y = K$ and $L_x + L_y = L$; the respective production functions are $X = X (K_x, L_x)$ and $Y = Y (K_y, L_y)$. In the lower left-hand corner of the Edgeworth Box, all inputs would be used for the production of Y and none for X. Moving toward the upper right-hand corner would shift resources from the production of Y to the production of X. Output levels of the two goods are represented by the production isoquants $X_1, X_2, ... X_n$ and $Y_1, Y_2, ... Y_n$. One of the key rationales for privatization is, of course, that public enterprises do not employ input factors efficiently, which is illustrated by the starting point **A** where the capital-labor ratio is not equal to the input price ratio –w/r. Since privatization is assumed to instill the profit motive, both firms have an incentive to reduce total cost by adjusting their input mixes. By doing so, the economy can increase total output (given inputs and technology) and move from point **A** to point **C**. Privatization therefore implies that the economy moves toward the production possibility frontier, leading to a one-time increase in overall output.

Whether the increase in productive efficiency is Pareto optimal depends on whether point **C** fulfills the condition of welfare maximization. With a single representative consumer, this condition is fulfilled where the PPF is tangent to the indifference curve, that is, the marginal rate of transformation is equal to the marginal rate of substitution.[26] Deviations from such an optimum are, however, not due to privatization per se but to market imperfections such as monopolies. Although profit-maximizing private owners are likely to pursue monopoly power more vigorously than their public counterparts, this does not represent an argument against privatization but rather a call for the establishment of adequate antitrust regulation in conjunction with privatization. Since this study focuses on the economic effects that can be attributed to privatization, issues of competitiveness are neglected. In the diagram above, it is assumed that point **C** is a welfare-maximizing bundle at which the indifference curve is tangent to the price ratio.

---

[26] It is assumed that the axioms of consumer choice are fulfilled and that consumer are utility-maximizing.

Figure 2.1. Privatization and Increases in Output

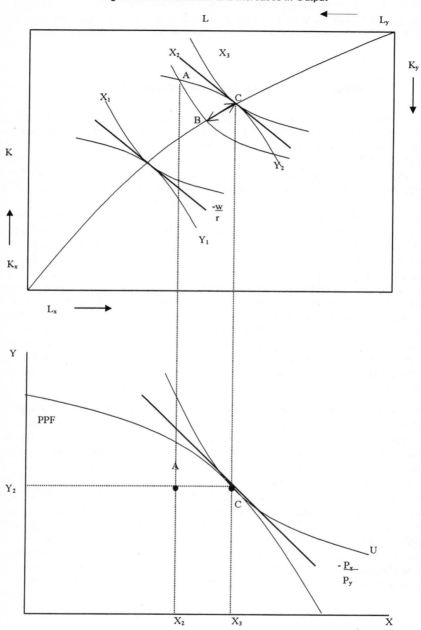

Such a static approach neglects, however, the fact that any adjustment will not occur instantaneously. The Edgeworth Box framework abstracts from imperfections in labor and capital markets. It is usually taken for granted that efficiency improvements on the firm level are by themselves sufficient to ensure that the economy at large moves closer to the production possibilities frontier. This would occur if a privatized company were to reallocate its resources and employ them more efficiently, thereby increasing output. Alternatively, the company might just dismiss idle resources and move to point **B**, producing the same quantity of X at lower cost. If the freed resources are used to increase the production of the other good, Y, aggregate output will still increase. However, industry Y may also adjust its input mix slightly, continuing to produce the same level of output at lower cost (point **C**), and leaving the remaining resources unemployed. In this case, total output in the economy would remain unchanged.

Only if labor and capital markets are efficient would overall output increase. Boycko, Schleifer, and Vishy (1993) point out that privatization might even lead to a decline in output if prior to privatization the government forced state-owned enterprises to maintain inefficiently high output levels. The question of whether and how quickly privatization will lead to an increase in output therefore depends on the institutional structure of both labor and capital markets.

2.2.1   Labor markets

On the firm level, privatization is likely produce increases in labor productivity. In cases where public enterprises pursued multiple objectives, such as maintaining high levels of employment, privatization will reinvigorate the profit motive and lead managers to cut costs by downsizing the workforce.[27] These improvements in technical efficiency are a necessary but not a sufficient condition for ensuring an increase in aggregate output. Rigidities and imperfections in factor markets may impede the shedding of extra resources, preventing firms from achieving technical efficiency. Even when firms are able to improve their efficiency, factor market imperfections will prevent the reemployment of these resources in other industries. Under these circumstances the primary effect of privatization is to convert "hidden" unemployment into open unemployment. [28]

---

[27] For an overview of the implications of different forms of firm ownership on technical or x-efficiency see Tirole (1988).

[28] Governments will have incentives to keep the political cost of unemployment to a minimum. As Boycko, Shleifer, and Vishny indicate, "there is nothing magic about privatization: just as the politician was willing to give up profits of a public firm on labor spending, he is willing to subsidize a privatized firm to 'buy' excess labor spending". (Boycko, Shleifer, and Vishny 1994, 2) Although they then present a model in which the separation of the firm from the government leads to a reduction in the workforce and hence improvements in efficiency, governments are likely to keep the macroeconomic effects of unemployment to a minimum which implies that increases in efficiency will remain below their potential. See also the section on employment issues of privatization.

Unless privatization is accompanied by institutional changes in the labor market, the absorption of freed resources is impaired and privatization might lead only to a fall in the equilibrium employment rate. An economy that had almost full employment prior to privatization is likely to experience higher equilibrium rates of unemployment afterward.

On the one hand, the transfer of ownership to the private sector will lead to a higher rate of frictional unemployment since the elimination of lifetime employment in the public sector will result in more search unemployment at any given time. Although this will to some extent be the cost of a more dynamic private sector vis-a-vis a more stagnant public one and not be limited to the short run, governments can minimize a surge in the frictional rate of unemployment by encouraging labor market mobility and an improvement in the flow of job information.[29] An increase in the search cost at a given wage rate would also imply that some groups will drop out of the labor market altogether. In particular, the labor market participation rate of women in the former socialist countries might be affected adversely.[30]

On the other hand, it is also reasonable to assume that involuntary structural unemployment increases at equilibrium and that the labor market will not clear at the going wage rate. The degree of involuntary unemployment will depend on institutional aspects such as bargaining rules; restrictions on the ability of private firms to hire and fire, for example, in the form of legally mandated job security; and the right to unemployment compensation and severance payments (on the last, see also the section on unemployment and severance payments). The fact that governments imposed employment objectives on their public enterprises in the first place is probably indicative of the institutional shortcomings of the labor market.[31] The mere freeing of excess labor resources will not be sufficient to increase output, implying that labor market reforms need to go hand-in-hand with privatization itself. The same would hold if, in the aftermath of privatization, the labor market participation rate were to decline.

2.2.2   Privatization and the financial system

Besides labor market constraints, a swift absorption of freed resources is also retarded if financial institutions are underdeveloped or faced with an incentive structure that leads to a suboptimal allocation of resources. Such a phenomenon is especially prevalent in developing countries and former socialist economies.

On the one hand, specialized human and physical capital will become obsolete at given input prices in the process of privatization and will require upgrading before

---

[29] The potential for a reduction in the natural rate of unemployment by the government is certainly limited. With respect to a reduction in information costs, the government could, for example, encourage contact between enterprises and educational institutions such as universities. Although quite common in countries like the US, in most developing countries the institutional barriers between educational institutions and business are quite large.

[30] See also Klassen (1994).

[31] See MacHale (1995).

it can be re-utilized. On the other hand, the establishment of an entrepreneurial private sector with the capacity to absorb large quantities of the privatization-related unemployed requires new capital in the form of bank loans, equity capital, and start-up venture capital. Since capital markets in many countries are non-existent or underdeveloped, commercial banks will initially have to play a central role in channeling financial capital to emerging sectors. There are various reasons why banks might not fulfill their role as efficient financial intermediaries. As long as banks themselves continue to be owned by the state, political objectives might play a more important role than profit maximization in the allocation of savings. Even privatized banks might not change their behavior immediately, as long as they continue doing business on the assumption that they will be bailed out if they fail. In both cases, banks might continue to make loans to large loss-making state-owned enterprises. After all, it is the profitable enterprises that get sold to the private sector, leaving the huge loss-makers in the hand of the state (see also fiscal issues of privatization). Since such behavior will crowd out private sector investment, the development of an entrepreneurial sector will be constrained. To ensure that the private sector has access to adequate resources, the government might need to implement credit ceilings for its large loss-making enterprises.

As in the case of labor market inefficiencies, capital market imperfections may prevent firms from achieving the resource balance needed to increase efficiency. Even when individual firms are able to move toward the production possibilities frontier (PPF), the same might not hold for the economy at large; improvements in efficiency at the firm level may not be translated into economy-wide increases in efficiency.

While the lack of a developed and efficient financial system prevents the swift reallocation of resources freed in the process of privatization, divestment is often mentioned as a means of improving the development of capital markets. The existence of developed capital markets is in turn assumed to correlate positively with economic growth and development.[32] A study by Megginson and Netter (1998) shows that privatization has indeed contributed substantially to the development of capital markets, improving both the depth and breadth of the markets. Based on publicly traded firms listed in the "Business Week Global 1000" and "Top 100 Emerging Market Companies," this study finds that the market capitalization of the privatized firms amounts to about 10 percent of the total market capitalization of all the firms contained in these two lists. Given that some 420 companies in the Global 1000 are U.S. firms while almost no large-scale privatizations took place in the U.S., the share of market capitalization increases to about 20 percent when U.S. firms are excluded.

---

[32] For a survey of the literature on financial repression and the implications on growth see, for example, Roubini and Sala-i-Martin (1995).

2.2.3   How do enterprises perform after privatization?

Concerning efficiency improvements as a result of privatization, a number of quantitative studies focus on improvements in the operational efficiency and profitability of individual firms. Overall, the studies seem to suggest that the financial performance of companies improves as a result of privatization. For example, in a broad survey study covering some 61 enterprises from 18 countries that were either partly or fully privatized through public share offerings, Megginson, Nash, and Van Randenborgh conclude that:

> Our results document strong performance improvements, achieved surprisingly without sacrificing employment security. Specifically, after being privatized, firms increase real sales, become more profitable, increase their capital investment spending, improve their operating efficiency, and increase their work forces (Megginson, Nash, and Van Randenborgh 1994, 403).

However, some indicators suggest that the performance of privatized enterprises is not meeting expectations. For example, Figure 2.2 shows the performance of European privatized entities that are publicly traded. The Morgan Stanley Composite Index (MSCI) is a broad market index that covers about 600 companies in the European Union, excluding Greece and Luxemburg but including Norway and Switzerland. The index of privatized companies covers all companies that were previously publicly owned and are traded on the stock exchange. While the performance of privatized companies has picked up since mid-1996, the overall relatively poor performance of the privatized entities might be related to the fact that the restructuring of these entities is lagging.[33]

In cases where the empirical evidence seems to point to a correlation between ownership and profitability, several caveats exist that caution against making inferences to improvements in the efficiency of the economy at large. Profitability is, of course, a poor proxy for efficiency. When control variables are included in a regression analysis to account for changes in the competitive environment, the adverse impact of privatization on allocative efficiency is not fully captured. Even in an existing industry structure, that is, without changes in the regulatory environment, profit-maximizing private entities are likely to have stronger incentives than their public counterparts to take advantage of market imperfections such as monopolies. After all, a key justification from a theoretical point for the existence of public enterprises was the assumption that public enterprises could implement pricing strategies that would take into consideration social marginal costs (Shapiro and Willig, 1990).[34] Furthermore, privatized firms might also be

---

[33] The author would like to thank Richard Davidson from Morgan Stanley Dean Witter for the provision of the data.

[34] La Porta and López-de-Silanes (1999) in a study on privatization in Mexico try separate the components that contributed to a higher ratio of operating income to sales after privatization. They estimate that 5 percent can be attributed to higher product prices, 31 percent a transfer from laid-off workers and the remainder can be attributed to productivity gains.

Figure 2.2. Performance of Privatized Enterprises in Europe, 1985-99

Index
(January 1985 = 100)

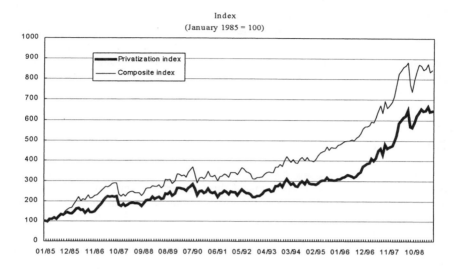

Relative Performance of Privatized Enterprises

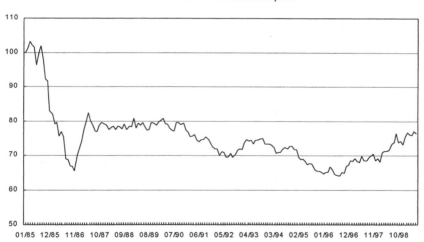

Sources: Morgan Stanley Dean Witter Data Base. 1999.

inclined to lobby more vigorously for regulatory changes that restrict competition. Another shortcoming relates to selection bias among industries chosen for privatization. For political reasons, governments are likely to select enterprises that will almost certainly be more profitable in the private sector. It is not surprising that the first enterprises to go are often those that operate in imperfect markets, such as airlines and telephone companies. Enterprises that should be liquidated, such as shipyards, and those that should be sold at scrap value are usually not among the prime candidates for privatization. The freeing of the resources in these enterprises would ensure the potential for major efficiency increases.

2.3   Social security and privatization

Recently, privatization has been mentioned in conjunction with the need to reform public pension systems. Proponents of this step argue that privatizing pension systems will raise national savings, thereby increasing investment and economic growth. Thus, this represents another area in which privatization may be associated with improved economic growth performance.

Most public pension system are defined-benefit systems that tax the current working generation to finance those who are retired.[35] The fact that pension systems are unsound in many industrialized countries has been documented in a number of studies. In Chand and Jaeger's (1996) simulations, for example, five out of a list of eight industrialized countries[36] are projected to show negative net asset positions as early as 2010; the net asset position of the remaining three countries, the United States, France, and Sweden, is projected to turn negative within the projection horizon that ends in 2050. The depth of the pension crisis is particularly extreme in the case of Germany, where the contribution rate would have to jump from about 23 percent of GDP in the year 1995 (defined as the rate that maintains year-by-year fiscal balance) to over 40 percent of GDP in 2030 in order to ensure the soundness of the system. The ratio of contributors to beneficiaries is expected to decline from 2.3 to 1.2 within the same period.[37]

Without changing the general nature of public pension systems, a number of reform measures are feasible to prevent the pension systems from going bankrupt or taxation from increasing to unsustainable levels. Among other things, these reforms would entail a reduction in benefits, either by reducing the replacement ratio, that is, the average benefits as a percent of average gross wages, or by modifying

---

[35] For a general overview of social security reforms see World Bank (1994), Siebert (1998) and Gruber and Wise (1997). For pension systems and reforms in transition economies see Cangiano, Cottarelli, and Cubeddu (1998).

[36] The countries are the United States, Japan, Germany, France, Italy, United Kingtom, Canada, and Sweden.

[37] See Leibfritz et.al. (1995) and VDR (1995).

automatic indexation mechanisms.[38] In addition, the pension age could be increased. Proponents of private pension systems argue that the current crisis of the public system calls for the creation of private pension systems based on defined contributions rather than defined benefits. Such a switch would ensure that politicians would have less of an impact on pensions and by definition would ensure that the system is sound, since benefits are tied to contributions at all times. From a macroeconomic perspective, privatization would be called for only if it led to higher savings and ultimately more economic growth.

One of the first proponents of privately administered and fully funded pension schemes, Feldstein (1974), argues that a pay-as-you-go system reduces national savings and economic growth and is associated with deadweight losses.[39] The impact on national saving is based on the notion that when a public pay-as-you-go system is introduced, the first generation enjoys a windfall profit as long as the expected present value of future benefits exceeds the expected present value of contributions. This will occur if the first generation qualifies for full benefits after having contributed only a few years. If the first generation considers this to be an increase in wealth, but at the same time the working generation whose contributions finance the pensions of the first generation considers their contributions as forced savings rather than a tax, overall private savings would fall. Such an assumption implies that current and future workers do not distinguish between the component of their contribution that represents the intergenerational transfer and the portion that determines their own pension. (Feldstein estimates that in the case of the United States, two thirds of the contribution rate represents transfers and only one third represents saving in that it will attract an adequate rate of return). Although the intergenerational transfer would only occur once, the capital stock would be permanently lower.[40]

---

[38] Such an adjustment might also be warranted if the indices that are currently being used overstate inflation. In the U.S., for example, the Boskin commission came to the conclusion that the CPI overstates the loss in the standard of living by about 1 percentage point. See Hulton (1997). Hence, adjusting pension payments by less than 100 percent of the change in the CPI would not necessarily imply a loss in real purchasing power.

[39] The arguments concerning the need for a reform of the social security system in the U.S. are nicely summarized by Feldstein (1996). Although he refers to the U.S., the arguments are representative for pay-as-you go systems in general.

[40] The implications of such an intergenerational transfer could best be exemplified by assuming that at time t, the government decides to give those who turn 65 years in time t a pension. For simplicity it is assumed that the qualifying generation has not made any prior contributions and that the pension is only offered to this generation. Future generations would still be required to make their own provisions for retirement. The establishment of such a pension arrangement would implicitly increase the liabilities of the government. Under such an arrangement, there should be no impact on saving since all that has taken place is an intergenerational transfer: the increase in consumption by the group of retired people is matched by higher taxes of the working generations. Since these do not aquire any pension rights, they are likely to perceive their payments as taxes and would reduce consumption accordingly. It is only when the current and future working generations acquire pension rights as well, so that their contributions combine a component of transfers to the

The privatization of a public pay-as-you-go system could have positive macroeconomic effects in the form of higher economic growth if the switch to a fully funded private system is associated with an increase in the national saving rate. However, privatizing a pension system is not necessarily synonymous with higher national saving. Assuming other things equal, the shift to such a private system would imply that the government continues making payments to current retirees but no longer receives contributions, which would lead to higher budget deficits and a fall in public saving. At the same time, however, the newly established private pension fund or funds would run surpluses since pension contributions would initially not be matched by any outlays. Overall, national savings would be unaffected. Kotlikoff argues that "if privatization ends up placing larger fiscal burden on initial older generations, it will lower the fiscal burden not only of the initial young, but also of all future generations" (Kotlikoff 1996, 5). His assumption of higher national savings as a result of privatization is predicated on two assumptions: first, that older generations have a higher propensity to consume out of remaining lifetime resources and second, that a system can be implemented that would reduce consumption of the older generation. While he shows that the propensity to consume is indeed higher for older generations and the imposition of a consumption tax would hence impact the older more than the younger generation, the consumption tax could be implemented whether or not the pension system is privatized.

Potential effects on national saving are probably more indirect. Due to the re-distributive nature of most public pension systems, the return of high income earners tends to be less than that of low income earners, which implies that the relatively higher payroll tax for high income earners is likely to have an adverse impact on their labor supply. Switching to a private fully funded system brings contributions and benefits in line, which should eliminate this labor market distortion and in turn increase the supply of labor. Privatizing a public system would therefore be associated with higher output, savings, and investment. In addition, national saving could also increase since public pension systems are more prone to payroll tax evasion than their privately administered counterparts. Depending on the design, under a defined benefit system people are likely to have incentives to avoid taxation.

By the same token, under certain circumstances privatizing a public system can also lead to a fall in the national saving rate. Among other things, if the privatized system offers a higher return than the public one, privatization could be associated with an increase in wealth, which would lead savings to fall. In any event, it seems that the net effects of privatizing a public pension system on saving and therefore on growth are ambiguous. Mackenzie, Gerson, and Cuevas (1997) come to the conclusion that if increasing the national saving rate is the objective of public policy, this could equally well be done, assuming Ricardian equivalence does not hold, by reforming a public pension system through either increasing payroll taxes or reducing retirement benefits, that is, through fiscal consolidation.

---

current retirees plus a pension right for themselves, that they might interpret the contributions as forced saving altogether.

The privatization of the Chilean system has become the benchmark for many pension reforms. In 1981, Chile switched from a public pension system with defined benefits to a privately administered but government-regulated defined contribution system.[41] Since the privatization of the Chilean pension system, other countries have followed suit. In the Western Hemisphere, countries such as Argentina, Bolivia, Colombia, El Salvador, Mexico, and Peru have started to privatize their social security systems over the last couple of years, albeit to varying degrees; in 1999, Poland became the first Eastern European country to adopt a Chilean-style pension system.[42] Since Chile has also enjoyed high growth rates, averaging almost 7 percent per annum from 1984 to 1995, the question arises whether the privatization of the pension system has contributed to higher private saving. Holzman's analysis of the Chilean case suggests that:

the data indicate that net pension savings were negative until 1989 and small afterward. These approaches independently suggests that the conventionally assumed impact of a Chilean-type pension reform on private (and national) saving may not hold (Holzman 1997, 175).

Instead he argues that the impact on growth took place more indirectly through the elimination of negative externalities (for example, the elimination of labor market distortions) and the creation of positive externalities such as the deepening of financial markets. These externalities in turn have a positive impact on total factor productivity, capital formation, savings, and growth. Privatizing pension systems are hence not likely to be a free lunch.

Policymakers who intend to increase savings and growth still have to undertake tough and often politically costly measures in the form of fiscal adjustment. These adjustments can take place either by reducing social security benefits and/or increasing contributions or by consolidating the public sector in general. In the case of Chile, for example, the government ran large primary fiscal surpluses to finance the benefits of existing retirees and to reduce the debt associated with the old pension system. However, at the time of privatization, Chile was ruled by the military government of Pinochet. Under a democratically elected regime, the constraints might have been quite different.

One of the key advantages of a system that has been privatized appears to be more related to political economy arguments, since a private and fully funded pension system isolates benefits somewhat from political considerations. For example, politicians might be inclined to make promises about future benefits at a time when government resources are temporarily abundant or to shift the burden of today's higher benefits and higher consumption to future generations that are absent from today's political decision making. The separation of such political considerations could, however, be implemented in the context of a public pension system if rules guaranteed the actuarial soundness of the pay-as-you go system at all times. Such rules could, for example, be established at the constitutional level. Also, from a political economy viewpoint, it has been argued that since switching to a private

---

[41] See Diamond and Valdés (1994).

[42] See Rodríguez (1999) and Salomon Smith Barney (1998).

pension system will initially lead to publicly visible higher fiscal deficits, politicians might be able to use the deterioration in the fiscal position to call for fiscal adjustments. Alternatively, they might be held accountable for a seemingly deteriorating fiscal position. Of course, the sale of public enterprises could also ease the transition to a fully funded system since the receipts could be used to capitalize it.

2.4   Summary

The fact that governments across the world have engaged in the divestment of public assets suggests that policymakers have bought into a new paradigm that minimizes the role of the government as a means of fostering economic growth. While the government's role has been curtailed in industrialized, former socialist economies and many developing countries, the financial crisis in South-East Asia has sped up the process of privatization even in that part of the world and potentially undermined the East Asian model of development.

Empirical studies tend to support the hypothesis that countries that rely on private ownership and private sector production of goods and services exhibit growth performance superior to that of countries that rely more heavily on the public sector. Given this empirical evidence, one would expect a reduction of government activity to be associated with improvements in the growth potential of the economy. To what degree this takes place depends on many factors: in addition to the size and execution of the privatization program, these factors include whether privatization leads to a more efficient use of available resources, how it affects the national savings and investment rate, and whether it stimulates technological progress.

In terms of the profitability of privatized enterprises, a majority of studies suggest that divestments are associated with an improvement in the profitability of the respective enterprises. However, a number of studies also show that profitability does not increase or the effects on profitability are unclear. The index for privatized enterprises in Europe confirms this view, given that the performance of the divested entities lags behind that of other publicly traded companies. Even in the case where profitability has improved after privatization, caution is warranted. In order to make the privatization program more publicly acceptable, governments may be inclined to privatize those entities that are most likely to generate higher profits after privatization. Furthermore, the improvement in profitability might also come at the price of a deterioration of allocative efficiency, given that private entities are likely to exploit market imperfections more effectively than their public counterparts. Privatized and profit-maximizing companies might also be more successful in securing restrictions on market entry.

Given that many pension systems are projected to be insolvent at current contribution and benefit rates, the call for the privatization of pension systems has become more forceful. The advantages of fully funded pension system are potentially numerous. They include the fact that benefits and contribution rates are not a function of political considerations, since benefits would by definition be tied to contributions. However, the assumption that the privatization of a pay-as-you-go system goes hand-in-hand with an increase in national savings and therefore economic growth is less clear-cut. The empirical evidence in the case of Chile seems to suggest that any positive growth impacts might have occurred more indirectly via the deepening of financial markets rather than through increasing national savings.

3 The Politics of Privatization

As indicated in the previous section, the decision to privatize should be guided by whether privatization is likely to raise national welfare and living standards. Most discussions on privatization suggest that policymakers are indeed primarily motivated by a desire to improve economic efficiency and growth. For example, Mark Baker from Privatization International suggests that:

> There can be no doubt ... that the once prevalent view of privatization as an exclusively right-wing ideology has shown itself to be shortsighted and ill informed. Practically every administration in the world has now embraced the principles of rationalization and efficiency that the majority of contributors to this book give as the major objective in transferring state-owned companies to the private sector (Baker, 1998: 1).

Such a statement is corroborated by the fact that divestment is pursued in almost every single country of the world and has become a universal phenomenon. It also reflects the fact that most politicians and policymakers use the efficiency argument to justify privatization and to gain popular support for their divestment programs.

However, the mere fact that privatization is pursued across countries and governments with different party platforms and ideologies warrants some caution. The assumption that governments engage in privatization primarily for efficiency reasons implies that politicians and policymakers are above all concerned about the maximization of welfare, that their own objective function coincides with that of the society at large, and that governments have largely bought into the neoclassical model.

Indeed, there are some reasons to believe in the occurrence of a systematic and widespread change in government behavior. Some governments might have learnt from their past mistakes and as a result changed their policies. Also, the globalization of international trade and capital has limited governments' ability to pursue policies that are deemed unfavorable or unsustainable by market participants, prompting policymakers to engage in economic reforms.[43] In particular, as a result of the integration of capital markets, investors can punish governments that pursue "bad" economic policies, as exemplified by the Mexican

---

[43] On the argument of the diminishing role of national governments as a result of globalization see also Tanzi (1998).

and East Asian financial crises. The integration of national economies into the world economy not only raises the cost of pursuing unsustainable policies but also makes it more difficult to exploit such policies for short-term political reasons. The more open national economies are, the more likely it is that their governments are constrained from pursuing short-term political objectives. For example, in an empirical study on political business cycles in developing countries, Schulknecht (1996) finds that closed economies exhibit strong fiscal cycles—that is, periods of increasing fiscal deficits before elections—while open and outwardly oriented economies do not.

However, although it is possible that governments have become more concerned with encouraging economic efficiency and growth, they still retain other objectives, such as the desire to win reelection or reward loyal follows. Since these objectives influence other areas of policymaking, it is likely that they also play a part in privatization decisions. Therefore, from a political economy viewpoint, it seems improbable that growth and efficiency arguments provide the sole motive for privatization.

The literature on the political economy of macroeconomic policymaking tries to explain why and under what circumstances politicians pursue policy objectives that are suboptimal from an economic welfare point of view. This literature can provide some guidance as to why governments might engage in privatization for political reasons in ways that are inconsistent with improving efficiency and growth.

3.1   Political-economy theories of macroeconomic policymaking

3.1.1   Delayed reforms and unsustainable policies

One topic that has been analyzed in the political economy literature is the question of why governments either delay economic reforms or embark on unsustainable policies in the first place. Of course, policymakers could disagree about the working model of the economy or about the appropriate policy response to, for example, an exogenous shock. Also, there might be different views about the appropriate timing and sequencing of economic reforms. However, if it is true, as suggested above, that most policymakers have bought into the same largely neoclassical model, one would assume that privatization is undertaken to increase efficiency and growth. Since privatization would produce an improvement in the standard of living of a large part of the population, privatization-minded politicians in turn should be rewarded with re-elections. However, as with many other economic reform measures, such as fiscal adjustments to increase national savings, trade and price liberalization to improve resource allocation, the tightening of monetary policy to reduce inflation, and exchange rate devaluations to improve competitiveness, privatization is likely to have undesirable effects on output and unemployment in the short term.[44] While the long-run benefits are likely to exceed any short-term costs, the reform government might not be in power long enough to reap the fruits of the long-run impact of privatization on economic welfare. Thus, potential long-run benefits may play only a limited role in policy decisions.

The tendency of governments to delay economic reforms or to embark on economic policies that are deemed unsustainable has been observed in industrialized and developing countries alike. For example, the reluctance of the British government to devalue its currency resulted in the crisis of the European Exchange Rate Mechanism (ERM) in 1992[45]. Also, even though public debt-to-GDP ratios rose over the past few decades in most industrialized countries, until very recently governments failed to address the underlying fiscal issues, resulting in ever-higher public debt-service payments.[46] In the case of developing countries, Rodrik (1996), in a review article on economic policy reform, uses the case of Peru during the administration of President Garcia to illustrate his argument that governments often engage in policies that initially lead to a "boom" but that are ultimately bound to end in a big "bust". He points out that, despite the large welfare costs at the end of the cycle, Garcia's economic program received great popular support.

Besides political economy explanations that assume myopia on part of the voting public, a number of models have been developed that assume rationality. These models are usually based on the assumption of asymmetric information or co-ordination problems among the respective groups.[47]

---

[44] Rodrik (1996), however, argues that the empirical evidence that reforms lead to adverse short-term impacts is sketchy. He mentions, for example, how disinflation policies through the adoption of exchange rate anchors quickly led to a resumption of growth in countries such as Argentina, Israel, and Mexico. He argues that the evidence on structural reforms suggests that growth performance improves only two to three years after the reform is implemented. Also, while there are similarities between privatization and other economic reforms, divestment differs in one fundamental way. For example, once a government has decided to remove price controls the resulting change in relative prices will eventually lead to an improvement in the allocation of resources. In a similar vein, a political decision to reduce trade barriers such as tariffs will ultimately increase competition, fostering efficiency and growth. In both cases and from a political economy point of view, the critical question is how to get politicians to move to economic reforms given the potentially politically costly adverse short-term implications. In the case of privatization, the decision to move forward does not necessarily coincide with an improvement in efficiency afterward but will still depend on the prime objectives for choosing to privatize in the first place. Again, unlike in the case of most other economic reforms, the motivation for divestment can be multifold and some of the objectives might not necessarily be compatible with an improvement in the structure of the economy, especially if the prime objective of the government is to raise domestic or external financing. The latter might be more consistent with a delay in economic reform rather than a change in the structure of the economy.

[45] For a brief discussion of the causes of the pressure on the British pound see Hayashi 1999.

[46] On rising debt-to-GDP ratios see Alesina and Roubini (1997): 228.

[47] See, for example, Alesina and Drazen (1991)

3.1.2   Political business cycles

A related phenomenon that has been analyzed and is potentially useful in explaining the enthusiasm for privatization relates to political business cycles.[48] For macroeconomic variables to play a crucial role in elections requires that voters consider macroeconomic conditions in their decision-making process. Some evidence suggests that this is the case and that incumbent parties and governments profit from a healthy rate of growth and low unemployment prior to elections. At the same time, incumbents are punished by voters if an election is preceded by a recession.[49]

The fact that macroeconomic conditions can be a decisive factor during elections has led to a number of theories on political business cycles. The underlying assumptions of such models are that politicians can influence short-term macroeconomic aggregates in a predictable direction and that voters actually cast their votes based on the state of the economy prior to the election. Depending on the assumption about the behavior of voters, the models are either part of the pre-rational tradition or fall into the group of rational-expectations models. Most models abstract from institutional details through which economic policy is conducted and merely assume that politicians can use monetary and fiscal policies to their ends. Irrespective of whether the models are of the pre-rational or rational kind, they assume a stable Phillips curve relationship between inflation—in the case of rational expectations, unexpected inflation—and economic output. Models of the political business cycle assume that politicians maximize their utility by getting re-elected and are based on a representative politician and indistinguishable voters. Hence, politicians have an incentive to use economic policy instruments to influence macroeconomic aggregates with the expectation that the economy will perform better shortly before an election.

Pre-rational models of the Nordhaus (1975) tradition explain political business cycles by arguing that an incumbent government undertakes expansionary fiscal or monetary policy prior to an election to prop up economic output and to reduce unemployment. Adverse impacts on inflation and government deficits are addressed after the election through monetary and potentially fiscal contractions. Such a strategy is, of course, only feasible if voters, being somewhat naïve about earlier states of the economy, cast their votes largely on the basis of the economic performance at the time of the election. More recent rational-electoral-cycle models assume that voters use all the available information efficiently in making their election decisions. On the basis of the available but incomplete information, they judge who would be most qualified to deal with exogenous shocks and to implement policies that foster long-term economic growth without inflation. While the assumption about the voter behavior differs from that of pre-rational models, the outcomes are somewhat similar in that policymakers can take advantage of asymmetric information to mislead voters, albeit not repeatedly.

---

[48] These models are sometimes also dubbed electoral-cycle or opportunistic models.

[49] See, for example, Lewis-Beck (1988) and Alesina and Rosenthal (1995).

The ability of policymakers to take advantage should be greater, the weaker the institutional system of checks and balances and the more discretionary power a government has in using fiscal and monetary policy instruments. While political business cycles have been observed in industrialized countries, the existence of such cycles should be especially pronounced in developing countries with weak political institutions, a proposition that appears to be supported by the empirical literature. [50]

3.1.3   Party platforms and economic policy

Another area of research has focused on whether political parties tend to manipulate macroeconomic aggregates such as inflation and unemployment according to their respective party platforms or "ideologies" and to reward their respective constituents once elected to office. Unlike political business cycle models, models of partisanship assume that parties are not totally opportunistic in their behavior, but differ in their pursuit of economic policies because of fundamental differences with respect to economic outcomes such as inflation, unemployment, and output. In other words, it is assumed that parties have different objective functions. Such differences in ideologies exist because parties cater to their respective constituencies, who are affected differently by economic outcomes. According to these models, one would expect that a more "right-wing" or "conservative" party would put more emphasis on reducing inflation than on reducing unemployment, while the reverse would be true for their "left-wing" counterpart. Once a party gets into office, it would then arrange to reach its optimal point on the Phillips curve. According to partisan models in the tradition of Hibbs (1977, 1987) one would hence expect "left-wing" parties to favor higher output at the expense of higher inflation, whereas "right-wing" parties would opt for lower output and inflation but at the cost of higher unemployment.

Alesina (1987) has augmented the models of partisanship by adopting the assumption of rational voters. As a result, his outcomes differ from those of traditional models of partisanship in that changes in output and unemployment as a result of changes in government are only temporary. In Alesina-type models, voters choose their party based on the respective party platform. Once a party gets into power, it will then undertake policies to please its constituencies. At the beginning of its term a "right-wing" party, for example, would reduce inflation. As a result, output would temporarily fall below its natural level, producing higher unemployment. In a model based on rational expectations, this is only possible because of asymmetric information between voters and elected officials, and in the case of Alesina's model, because of the assumption that nominal wage contracts are signed at discrete intervals that do not coincide with election dates. However, after expectations and all relevant prices have adjusted in the economy, the economy will again approach the natural level of output. As a matter of fact, Alesina argues that at the end of the adjustment period "the level of economic activity should be independent of the party in office" (Alesian, 1994: 44). If a "left-wing" party is in

---

[50] See Schulknecht (1996).

office, the natural level of output and unemployment would be associated with a higher inflation rate since the public anticipates that the government engages in expansionary policies to reduce unemployment. Since inflation is at a higher level, that is, the target level on the Phillips curve, the party has no incentive to continue with its expansionary policy and expected inflation is equal to the actual inflation rate. A number of studies find empirical evidence for the rational partisan theory both for the United States and other OECD countries.[51]

3.2   Government behavior and privatization

The degree to which political parties and politicians have an incentive to and can manipulate macroeconomic aggregates to foster their objectives or to postpone economic reforms will vary across countries and is likely to be a function of the country's institutional and political structure. For example, countries with a two-party system in which each party represents a clearly defined ideology such as "left wing" or "right wing" are more likely to engage in economic policies to reward their respective constituencies than countries that traditionally have coalition governments or a multiparty system. However, irrespective of these differences and hence the likely behavior of governments, the phenomena covered by the political economy literature can contribute to an understanding of why privatization has becomes such a popular instrument of public policy.

Traditionally, it is assumed that privatization reflects a change in the direction of economic policy on the part of policymakers. However, if the insights of the political economy literature are applied, privatization is compatible with unchanged government behavior and "business as usual". Governments that had an incentive to delay economic reforms or to pursue unsustainable policies can now—as a result of the paradigm change—employ privatization to such an end. For example, the tendency of governments in developing countries to engage in expansionary policies if temporary foreign financing is available but to resist implementing the necessary adjustments once the funding subsides can now be facilitated by the sale of public assets abroad.[52] In the same vein, governments that used standard fiscal and monetary policy to improve their chances of getting elected can now do so with the help of privatization receipts. Even those political systems that allowed political parties to reward their constituents with particular short-term macroeconomic outcomes once elected into office can use privatization for such an end.

The universal acceptance of privatization as a policy instrument has given politicians an opportunity to use privatization to pursue short-term objectives. While the stock of public assets lasts, divestment can be used in addition to traditional instruments such as fiscal and monetary policy. In some ways, divestment might even be superior to traditional policy instruments as a means of

---

[51] See Klein (1996) and Alesina and Rosenthal (1995).

[52] Ranis and Mahmood (1992), for example, show that a number of countries engaged in such spending sprees.

manipulating macroeconomic aggregates. Many aspects of privatization, such as its fiscal implications, lack transparency and are therefore difficult for the public to monitor due to high information costs. At the same time, financial markets and the public have gradually forced governments to provide more and timely data including information on public deficits and debt stock, monetary aggregates, and more recently—as a result of the latest financial crises—on the size and composition of international reserves. Public pressure has also contributed to institutional changes that have reduced the discretionary power of politicians and policymakers. Central banks across the globe have gained more independence, budgetary procedures are streamlined and the call for fiscal transparency has increased.[53] However, the sale of assets has largely been unaffected by those changes.

3.3   Summary

If politicians care primarily about getting re-elected and voters are guided in their voting behavior more by immediate and tangible results in the short term than by long-term economic developments, politicians have an incentive to engage in policies that are expected to have positive short-term effects on the economy. At the same time, governments have an incentive to abstain from reforms that cause economic hardship in the short term. Alternatively, newly elected governments might have an incentive to engage in specific policies, such as a reduction in inflation, to reward particular interest groups. As the above-mentioned models on the politics of macroeconomic policymaking demonstrate, such "short-term" behavior can be explained irrespective of whether one assumes "rational" behavior on the part of the voters or constituencies or short-sighted or naïve voters. It merely requires that policymakers assume that they can take advantage of a stable Phillips curve relationship between inflation and economic output.

Drawing on the political economy literature for the analysis of privatization may help explain why the world is experiencing the current wave of privatization without having to resort to the very heroic assumptions that politicians across the globe have changed their objective function, have universally embraced the neoclassical model, or become benevolent guardians. Therefore, the discussion about the macroeconomic aspects of privatization in the following chapters is guided by the insights of the politics of macroeconomic policymaking. Although the fiscal, monetary, balance-of-payments, and employment aspects are covered from both a normative and empirical perspective, the chapters also try to identify

---

[53] The Bank of England, for example, gained independence in 1997. For a number of countries such as Spain and France joining EMU implied a move toward more independence. On central bank independence and the performance of inflation see also Alesina and Summers (1993). The IMF, for example, has placed more emphasis on the adoption of fiscal policy rules by member countries. See for example Kopies and Craig (1996) and Kopies and Symansky (1998).

whether governments have engaged or are likely to engage in privatization for short-term political reasons.

4 Fiscal Considerations of Privatization

Despite the common perception—which in part reflects the success of policymakers and politicians in using efficiency arguments to advocate privatization—efficiency gains are only one possible motive for governments to engage in large-scale privatization. The following chapter examines the various circumstances under which fiscal considerations may instead provide incentives for privatization.

From a fiscal point of view, privatization should be undertaken only when it positively affects the long-run fiscal position of the government, as reflected in an improvement in the government's intertemporal budget constraint. Such an improvement will occur when efficiency gains from privatization increase the sales price of the privatized assets. However, given their limited time horizons, governments may instead be motivated primarily by short-run considerations. One possibility is that policymakers may use privatization as a means of influencing macroeconomic aggregates; the effectiveness of this strategy depends on whether the public's behavior can be explained by Ricardian equivalence. This chapter argues that a more important motive for privatization can be found in the opportunity for loosening the government's one-period budget constraint, without regard to whether this results in an improvement of the net wealth position of the government. Furthermore, it is shown that even industrialized countries with developed capital markets are inclined to engage in privatization largely for fiscal reasons.

4.1 The intertemporal budget constraint

To demonstrate the fiscal impact of privatization, the following uses the intertemporal budget constraint as a benchmark. The intertemporal budget constraint of the public sector requires that all government expenditures ultimately be financed through genuine revenues, which are usually thought of as tax and non-tax revenues as well as government grants. The traditional budget constraint for an infinite time horizon may be extended to incorporate privatization. Let the variable PED reflect the annual payments governments receive from their public entities in the form of dividends or transfers (or alternatively, the subsidies the government pays to loss-making entities). Then the following must hold:

$$\sum_{t=1}^{\infty} \frac{T_t}{(1 + r)^{t-1}} + \sum_{t=1}^{\infty} \frac{PED_t}{(1 + r)^{t-1}} = D_0 + \sum_{t=1}^{\infty} \frac{G_t}{(1 + r)^{t-1}}$$

where T stands for tax revenues, PED for dividend payments from public entities, D for the stock of public debt at the beginning of the period and G for government spending. If the government privatizes assets during period t, it will receive the sales price of those assets as part of PED at time t, then no further revenues from those particular assets. In general, the sales price should reflect the present discounted value of the expected stream of payments generated by the assets. In other words, through privatization, the government receives its revenues "up front" rather than as a infinite stream of payments equal in net present value.

The initial debt stock D—or at least a portion of it—represents the amount the government borrowed from the private sector for the initial establishment of the public sector entities. Therefore, the annual income (PED) the government receives represents service of this portion of its debt stock. Since the size of the initial borrowing is conceptually related to the expected future stream of income from the public sector assets, as a first approximation and assuming everything else equal, the divestment of public assets would leave the intertemporal budget constraint unchanged. Alternatively and in the aggregate, privatization implies that the government exchanges its ownership in public assets for a redemption of its previous debt. The intertemporal budget constraint would revert back to the standard form in which the net present value of taxes is equal to the net present value of all government spending. The intertemporal budget constraint demonstrates that governments should be largely indifferent to privatization, at least from a fiscal perspective.

This conclusion holds true even when the public assets are not profitable. Several studies point out that especially in developing countries, the poor performance of public entities caused governments to provide large subsidies that in turn are at the heart of large fiscal deficits. Floyd (1984) states, for example, that public enterprises accounted on average for 4 percent of GDP of government deficits in the 1970s. Furthermore, Pinheiro and Schneider (1994) show that public entities in Argentina, Brazil, and Mexico ran operational deficits of between 4 and 7 percent of GDP in 1982. Similar results were also true in former socialist economies. Earnst, et. al. (1996) show that government subsidies to Polish enterprises prior to economic transformation amounted to almost 7 percent of GDP in 1989. In principle, it appears that the privatization of loss-making enterprises would relieve the government from this fiscal burden and improve the government's net wealth position. However, the above-stated intertemporal budget constraint suggests otherwise. The mere sale of entities that are a drain on the public purse should leave the net wealth position of the government unchanged since, ceteris paribus, the government would have to assume the net present value of all losses reflected in the assumption of company debt prior to privatization.

A fiscal improvement would occur only if by divesting such entities the government is able to increase the net present value of dividend payments or decrease the net present value of future losses. For this to occur, the transfer of ownership to the private sector would have to be associated with an improvement in the efficiency of the respective entities as well as with the ability of the government to capture the improvement through higher sales prices.[54] An improvement in efficiency, however, also requires that governments abstain from imposing restrictions on the operation of the companies once they are in the hands of private investors. Under such circumstances, the maximization of privatization receipts for fiscal reasons would be compatible with the objective of improving efficiency and growth. However, as will be discussed in the section on employment, governments might have incentives to prevent private investors from achieving substantial increases in efficiency by imposing restrictions on, for example, the ability of new owners to reduce the workforce.

The poor performance of public enterprises is often a function of the public policy objectives imposed on these entities. Besides having a mandate to provide goods and services, such as water and electricity, at subsidized rates to particular social groups, public entities are often burdened with the mandate of functioning as employers of last resort. Under these circumstances, the mere act of privatization would not necessarily change the government's intertemporal budget constraint. If these entities are sold to private investors without such mandates, the profitability of these entities improves and $\sum_{t=1}^{\infty} \dfrac{PED_t}{(1 + r)^{t-1}}$ increases, leading to an improvement in the budget constraint as long as the government can capture the improvement through the collection of higher sales receipts. However, unless the government changes its overall public policy by reducing the provision of subsidized goods and services and scrapping employment guarantees, the increase in the net present value of the stream of dividend payments would be matched by an increase in direct government outlays, causing $\sum_{t=1}^{\infty} \dfrac{G_t}{(1 + r)^{t-1}}$ to increase accordingly. While privatization can be a vehicle for reducing government subsidies and the provision of other public services, the sale of assets by itself does not lead to an improvement in the net worth of the government.

In the example outlined above, the maximization of sales receipts was consistent with maximizing efficiency, although the achievement of both objectives could be

---

[54] To extract any expected improvements in efficiency, the government has to engage in market based privatization methods. On optimal privatization methods see Maskin 1992. Also, an outright undervaluation tightens the budget constraint. The most extreme impact on the net-wealth position of the government takes place in the case of voucher privatization. In this case the government provides coupons to particular groups—such as the entire adult population of a country—either free of charge or at a nominal fee. The voucher can then in turn be used to acquire shares in privatized companies. Since this amounts to a direct transfer of income and wealth, voucher privatization leads to a worsening of the net-wealth position of the government. On voucher privatization in eastern Europe see Lipton and Sachs (1990).

impeded by the requirements of public policy. However, in some cases the desire to maximize sales receipts actively conflicts with achieving efficiency goals. For example, private investors will be willing to pay more to receive the excess profits generated by monopolies. Thus, governments wishing to maximize sales receipts will have an incentive to grant monopoly rights to purchasers of privatized assets. Even in the case where public entities operated as monopolies prior to privatization,

the term $\sum_{t=1}^{\infty} \dfrac{PED_t}{(1+r)^{t-1}}$ should improve as a result of privatization, since private

operators are likely to exploit monopoly rights more aggressively than government bureaucrats. Again, assuming the associated increase in profitability is reflected in the sales price, the intertemporal budget constraint of the government improves. This time, however, the improvement is at the expense of allocative efficiency.

The preceding discussion demonstrates that privatization without any additional measures is likely to have only a marginal impact on the net worth of the government. This argument suggests that if fiscal considerations are defined as a desire to improve the government's intertemporal budget constraint, there is little evidence to support such considerations as a primary motive for privatization.[55]

5.2   Ricardian equivalence

Aside from the possibility of improving the government's net wealth position through privatization, fiscal considerations may provide a further motive for privatization if, by selling public assets, the government is able to influence macroeconomic aggregates in a desirable fashion. For example, revenues from asset sales could be used to finance additional government spending, increasing output and lowering unemployment. However, economic theory does not provide a clear answer as to the effectiveness of this strategy. Whether or not privatization has broader macroeconomic implications is—among other things—related to the behavior of economic agents. The discussion of whether and under what circumstances the public deficit has any impact on macroeconomic aggregates was revived by Barro (1974) in his extension of Ricardian equivalence. Barro suggested that it does not matter whether a given level of public expenditure is financed by collecting taxes or by running a deficit. Although the focus is on the equivalence of taxes and government borrowing, the argument could be expanded to include privatization if the assumption is made that the issue of government bonds and the sale of assets are identical. For example, a reduction in taxes today could be financed through either the issue of government debt or the sale of public assets. In either case the tax burden would only be shifted to future years.

In the case of privatization, future taxes would have to be raised to compensate for the forgone future income from the operation of public entities. In the hypothetical case that both households and the government have the same time horizon, a tax cut

---

[55] On fiscal issues of privatization see also Pinheiro and Schneider (1994).

in period one would prompt rational households to take precautionary measures in the form of higher savings to pay for the associated tax increase in the future. A decline in government savings would be matched by an equivalent increase in private savings, leaving the interest rate unaffected.[56] In essence, under the Barro-Ricardian assumption, government bonds—and analogously the purchase of equity stakes in public enterprises—would not be part of aggregate net wealth. However, for Ricardian equivalence to hold, a number of fairly heroic assumptions have to be made that are questionable both on theoretical and empirical grounds.

If economic agents are not infinitely lived, it must be shown that the assumption of a budget constraint for one generation also applies to the case of overlapping generations. Otherwise, the current generation would have the benefit of lower taxes but would be able to pass on the cost of debt repayment to future generations. Barro's argument that generations are linked through family ties leading to an altruistic bequest motive seems to be rather weak. While households might at least partly adjust their bequests to compensate for the additional tax liability of their children, it would be a very strong assumption that the current generation would fully adjust its consumption pattern as a result of privatization-induced tax reductions.

Furthermore, Ricardian equivalence only holds if capital markets are perfect. The depth of capital markets and hence the degree to which they approximate such an assumption varies to a large degree among countries, and it would be presumptuous to make such an assumption in the case of transition economies and developing countries. Frequently, the private sector in non-industrialized countries is precluded from borrowing abroad altogether. Furthermore, due to the risk of default and higher transaction costs, the discount rates are not likely to be identical in both the private and the public sector.[57] Since with a higher discount rate in the private sector, the present value of future taxes will be lower, households are likely to spend more. Also, households are often faced with liquidity constraints since, for example, the banking sector has little experience in evaluating assets as collateral and might continue to favor lending to the government or public enterprises, assuming that the latter will be bailed out if necessary. Liquidity-constrained households are likely to increase their consumption if they receive tax cuts.[58]

Besides the issue of overlapping generations and the assumption about perfect capital markets, Barro-Ricardian equivalence fails to hold if applied to the reality of national tax systems. Since national tax systems tend to be highly distortionary, a change in the rate of a particular tax will cause economic behavior to change. For example, a cut in income tax as a result of privatization is likely to increase the incentive to work, with repercussions for both the potential of economic growth and

---

[56] For a formal treatment of Ricardian equivalence see also Azariadis (1993).

[57] See Leiderman and Blejer (1988).

[58] See Buiter and Tobin (1979) as well as Hubbard and Judd (1986) on the liquidity constraint arguments.

the interest rate.[59] A related issue is the monetization of government debt. Although one could argue that the monetization of debt is just another form of taxation, it is rather likely that the groups who profit from tax cuts—high income earners in the case of income tax reductions—differ from those who have to carry the burden of the inflation tax. A change in inflationary expectations could therefore cause aggregate spending to increase.

Given that the underlying assumptions for the Barro-Ricardian equivalence are so stringent, a change in taxes as a result of privatization should allow governments to influence interest rates, aggregate demand, and the current account.[60] As in the case of government borrowing, a reduction in taxes today as a result of privatization should lead to an increase in aggregate demand, allowing governments to use privatization as a means of affecting output and unemployment in the short run.[61]

5.3   The one period budget constraint

The intertemporal budget constraint provides a normative guidepost for privatization: privatization is recommended when it improves efficiency, as reflected in an improvement in the government's net worth. However, governments also face a second budget constraint, which requires that in any given period all government spending must be financed. A change in paradigm that permits privatization effectively softens this one-period budget constraint by providing an additional temporary source of financing. This suggests an additional motive for privatization, one that, given the short-term focus of policymakers, may more adequately capture the political enthusiasm for privatization.

If G stands for government expenditure, T for taxes, BD for domestic non-bank borrowing, BF for foreign borrowing, $NDCG$ for net credit to the government from the banking system, and PR for privatization receipts, the one-period budget constraint can be expressed as follows:

$$G = T + BD + BF + NDCG + PR$$

The inclusion of PR in the equation gives policymakers an additional choice in pursuing their policy objectives, irrespective of whether or not privatization will affect the intertemporal budget constraint. Ceteris paribus, as a result of privatization policymakers can

- increase government expenditure on a temporary basis above and beyond what otherwise would be possible. If other sources of financing remain unchanged, an

[59] See also Lucas (1986), Aschauer and Greenwood (1985), as well as Frenkel and Razin (1987) on the argument of distortionary taxes and Ricardian equivalence.

[60] On the empirical irrelevance of Ricardian equivalence see also Altonji (1992) and Bernheim (1989).

[61] See also CBO (1989) for a brief overview of assumptions about the relationship between deficits and interest rates according to the various economic schools.

increase in government expenditure would allow governments to affect aggregate demand in a predetermined manner;

- maintain a level of expenditure—and hence avoid a politically adverse fiscal contraction—even in light of a shortfall in any of the other sources of financing;[62]

- lower taxes; besides re-distributional effects that allow governments to target politically influential groups in society, the government could use a privatization-financed reduction in taxes to stimulate aggregate demand. The latter, of course, requires that households are non-Ricardian;

- lower the recorded and publicly visible fiscal deficit by counting privatization receipts as a revenue equivalent, that is, as an above the line item.

Of course, in principle the above-listed budget identity does not indicate why a government is faced with a hard budget constraint and hence would resort to privatization. After all, it is only in the limit that a government is constrained from raising additional resources to finance its expenditure, since it can always raise taxes, take out more loans from the banking sector, issue more debt, and last but not least, resort to the inflation tax.[63]

Privatization becomes, however, attractive since most governments are constrained in one form or another, be it because of real budgetary constraints or because of political or institutional circumstances. For example, a government might

- not have access to voluntary foreign lending due to a previous default on sovereign debt as well as prior debt moratoria;

- be faced with prohibitively high domestic interest rates as a result of poor fiscal discipline, previous arrears or outright default on domestic debt;

- see itself unable to use seignorage because of recent experiences with high or hyperinflation. Furthermore, outside forces such as an IMF program might also limit the scope of using the printing press;[64] and

- be precluded from increasing tax revenues—at least in the short run—because of shortcomings of the tax system such as poor tax administration and collection or a narrow tax base. Reforming the tax system frequently yields results only after some years and can even lead to short-term revenue declines. With privatization as a financing option, raising taxes is certainly politically more

---

[62] This also includes the substitution of bank financing (NDCG), especially in developing countries and transition economies, that intend to lower their inflation rates without engaging in the required fiscal adjustment that would be necessary in the absence of privatization receipts. See also the section on monetary issues.

[63] In the short term, it can also resort to arrears as a means of financing.

[64] In some countries, seignorage was a relatively stable source of government revenue. In the case of Argentina, for example, seignorage was relatively stable over the 1970s. Ultimately, this came to a halt as a result of the two hyperinflations in 1989 and 1991.

costly and the government might perceive that an additional increase in tax rates will lead to their defeat in the next elections.

Besides any real constraints of not having access to voluntary foreign lending and the high fiscal costs of prohibitively high real interest rates, it is the politically perceived budget constraint that makes privatization such an attractive instrument for maintaining or even increasing expenditures.[65] After all, it appears that public opposition to using privatization as a means of financing is slight compared with other ways of increasing financial resources for the government. Both cuts in expenditure and increases in taxes are politically quite costly. Even government borrowing is often closely watched by the public and financial markets, and continued increases are likely to become politically unpopular once a certain threshold is passed. The sale of assets for fiscal reasons, however, appears to have little political cost, probably because the fiscal treatment of privatization is often not very transparent. Since intergenerational accounting and the concept of public sector net wealth are mostly academic concepts and are not reported by governments on a regular basis, a reduction in the stock of public assets is usually not recorded in a way that can easily be scrutinized by the public.[66] In cases where privatization receipts are treated as a tax equivalent, it even leads to a reduction in the publicly visible government sector deficit.[67]

The use of privatization receipts to overcome fiscal constraints would be negligible both for macroeconomic and political reasons, if the stock of divestable assets and hence the flow of receipts in the respective countries were small. However, as figure 4.1 and 4.2 show, industrialized and developing countries alike have engaged in massive divestment programs, leading to privatization receipts in excess of 4 percent of GDP in a given year. On a cumulative basis over the past 10 years, countries such as Argentina, Australia, and Hungary privatized assets worth more than 11 percent of GDP, while Denmark, Peru, Sweden, and the United Kingdom have divested assets of more than 7 percent of GDP. Worldwide, privatization receipts have reached cumulatively more than 2 percent of world GDP.

The magnitude of these privatization flows demonstrates the attractiveness of privatization as a means of temporarily financing government expenditure in countries that are faced with real financing constraints.[68] A well-documented case,

---

[65] The limit to foreign and domestic financing in a period of hyperinflation is also discussed in Dornbusch, Sturzenegger and Wolf (1990).

[66] For a brief overview of generational accounting see Leibfritz (1996).

[67] Such endeavors could even be found in economic programs that were supported by the IMF. Abdala states that "This is clearly revealed in the stand-by agreements that the government signed with the IMF in mid-1991. Proceeds from privatization are stated to be vital in meeting targeted primary budget surpluses during 1991-1992" (Abdala 1994: 466).

[68] Chile's privatization program preceded those in other countries that took place as a result of the general acceptance of privatization as a tool of fiscal policy in the 1980s. Nevertheless, it serves as an example of how fiscally motivated privatization can be at odds with the creation of viable privately run enterprises. In order to maximize privatization revenues, the government accepted offers from highly leveraged investors to acquire public entities between 1975 and 1979. As a result, the macroeconomic crisis at the beginning of the 1980s

Figure 4.1. Privatization Receipts: Industrialized Countries
(In percent of GDP 1/)

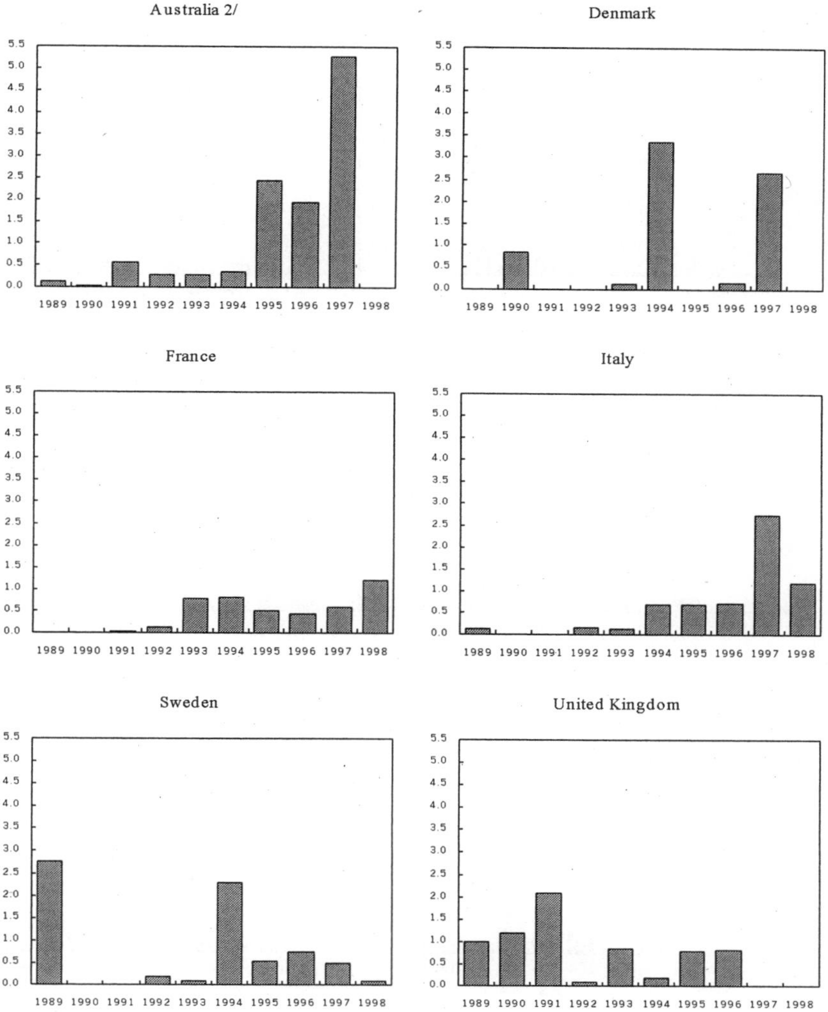

Sources: Privatization Yearbook (various issues); IMF (1999.1).

1/ GDP in U.S. dollars at PPP exchange rates.
2/ Data for 1998 not available.

resulted in widespread bankruptcies of these entities, prompting the government to assume control again and to absorb the fiscal cost (see Pinheiro and Schneider, 1994).

Figure 4.2. Privatization Receipts: Emerging Markets
(In percent of GDP 1/)

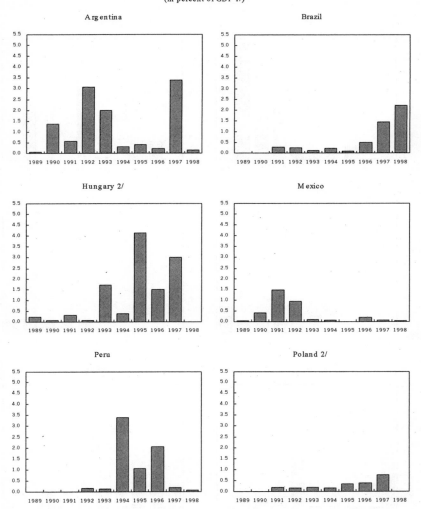

Sources: Privatization Yearbook (various issues); IMF (1999.1).

1/ GDP in U.S. dollars at PPP exchange rates.
2/ Data for 1998 not available.

for example, is Argentina. In the aftermath of two hyperinflations, the government had lost its ability to finance its operations and had practically lost access to any form of voluntary lending. Abdala points out that since Argentina was unable to generate current account surpluses to meet external interest payments and the government had already reached arrears of U.S. $5.4 billion (some 14 percent of commercial external debt), the government was no longer able to access external resources. Furthermore, since the marginal cost of domestic borrowing had reached almost 60 percent in U.S. dollar terms in 1989, the issue of domestic debt was also not a viable option and "did not significantly differ from inflationary finance in the sense that it failed to shift the burden of taxation further into the future" (Abdala 1994: 472). In order to maximize privatization receipts, the government provided monopoly rights to investors even in areas that could no longer be considered natural monopolies, such as telecommunications and commercial air cargo services. By doing so, it sacrificed the objective of improving allocative efficiency.[69]

Besides developing countries and transition economies, the hypothesis that budgetary constraints are a key determinant for privatization can even be supported in the case of the United States. Since public ownership in the United States on the federal level is limited, an analysis of the behavior of policymakers at lower levels of government is quite telling. López-de-Silanes, Schleifer, and Vishny (1995) test empirically whether counties that are faced with a hard budget constraint are more likely to privatize than those that lack such institutional constraints. They operationalize the assumption of a hard budget constraint by using dummy variables for whether state laws prevent counties from issuing short-term debt, impose debt ceilings or mandate balanced budgets. Furthermore, the study uses a variable that captures whether states have the possibility of bailing out counties that are in financial distress and whether counties have the ability to impose discretionary taxes. The study supports—in broad terms—the hypothesis that counties with hard budget constraints are more likely to resort to privatization than their counterparts without such constraints.[70]

While the hypothesis that fiscally constrained governments resort to privatization seems to be supported by both anecdotal and empirical evidence, it is less obvious why industrialized countries with developed capital markets would privatize for fiscal reasons. Again, it appears that political motives are paramount in explaining why this might be. Rising government expenditures and the general public's resistance to ever-higher tax rates caused fiscal deficits and public debt stocks to increase in many industrialized countries over the past decades.[71] Besides the potential crowding-out effect and the adverse impact on private sector activity—depending on the openness of the economy—large fiscal deficits and rising debt stocks are likely to get the attention of financial markets and voters. Since both groups are likely to question the long-run sustainability of such developments, it

---

[69] See, for example, Gerchunoff and Cánovas.(1994).

[70] In case of the balanced budget mandate and the variable capturing whether a county is able to impose discretionary taxes, the statistical evidence is, however, insignificant or the variable has the wrong sign.

[71] See Alesina and Roubini on debt-to-GDP ratios.

becomes opportune for policymakers to address these issues by calling for fiscal consolidation and a reduction in fiscal deficits.[72] While such public statements and a reduction in the publicly visible deficit are politically attractive, the required fiscal adjustments would be associated with a reduction in the provision of government goods and services or a reduction in government transfers and subsidies. Such real fiscal adjustments are likely to be politically unpopular, at least among the affected groups. Policymakers who try to maximize their votes, therefore, have an incentive to lower the publicly visible fiscal deficit without alienating voters and could be inclined to use privatization for such a purpose. While the use of privatization for such purposes would largely be an illusion, it would be in line with other government efforts to minimize the transparency of fiscal operations, for example by creating off-budget operations.

Evidence for such efforts can be found both in the United States and in European countries. In the case of the United States, such attempts were made in the context of deficit reduction based on the Gramm-Rudman-Hollings Act in the 1980s. Prior to the act—and largely as a result of tax cuts and increased defense spending—the United States budget deficit had increased steadily during the first half of the 1980s, reaching an all-time high of 6 percent of GDP in 1985. Since Congress and the Reagan Administration could not agree on how to confine the deficit, Senators Gramm, Rudman, and Hollings introduced a bill that envisioned balancing the Federal Budget by the year 1991.[73] According to the legislation—which became law in 1985—if no agreement could be reached between the Administration and Congress to achieve the predetermined deficit targets, automatic across-the-board spending cuts would take place.[74] The goal of the Act was to address the population's growing concerns about ever-rising deficits and debt stocks. Walters points out that part of the "deficit reduction" was accomplished through accounting illusions. He states that "some of the reduction in spending under the Gramm-Rudman-Hollings process is achieved by disposing of federally owned assets. Such measures are accounting delusions and should be abjured" (Walters, 1989).

The availability of public assets seems to be an instrument for governments to misguide the public and capital markets about the true fiscal stance of the public sector. The United Kingdom, for example, used privatization receipts to lower the publicly visible government-sector-borrowing requirement.[75] More recently, the deficit and debt reduction efforts by countries to meet the Maastricht criteria for joining the European Monetary Union (EMU) resulted in a privatization frenzy driven primarily by "fiscal reasons".

---

[72] In Germany, the term "Haushaltskonsolidierung" (budget consolidation) was even voted most popular word of the year in 1995.

[73] In addition, Congress readjusted the deficit targets several times, defeating the purpose of predetermining the deficit ceiling.

[74] On the political economy dimension of the Gramm-Rudman-Hollings Acts see also West (1988).

[75] See Vickers and Yarrow (1988).

Initially, countries such as Belgium attempted to meet the Maastricht deficit targets by applying privatization receipts toward such.[76] While in the end Eurostat ruled against the use of privatization receipts toward meeting the deficit criteria, countries continued to maximize fiscal receipts from privatization in order to lower debt stock targets and improve the fiscal deficit, at least at the margin, by lowering interest payments. For example, in the case of Belgium, the then-Prime Minister Dehaene indicated that

... the total debt-to-GDP ratio next year would be 127 percent, down from an estimated 130 percent at the end of 1996, assuming economic growth of 2.1 percent next year. He added the government will use 222 billion francs from sales of gold by the National Bank of Belgium to pay off debt, and another 70 billion franks of debt payments would be financed from selling public assets. A further 75 billion franks of debt would be paid from savings made from more effective management of financial assets. .... Dehaene said the budget ensures Belgium will comply with EU monetary union criteria, adding that the country is now a defacto member of EMU (IMF, October 2, 1996: 1).

The case of Belgium does not represent an exception to the rule but rather tends to confirm the rule.[77] The following example shows how Germany changed its privatization objectives over the years and how EMU influenced the government to push for massive privatization in West Germany.

4.4   Fiscal motives of large industrialized economies: privatization in Germany and EMU

4.4.1   Background

The outcome of World War II shaped the economic landscape of the two resulting Germanies: the former Federal Republic of Germany (FRG) and the former German Democratic Republic (GDR). Whereas in the east most enterprises were expropriated, nationalized, and converted into so-called "Volkseigene Betriebe" (VEBs), the west—which later became the Federal Republic of Germany (FRG)— opted for an economic model based principally on the provision of goods and services by the private sector.[78] The new state, however, inherited a large number of public enterprises that had been founded in earlier years. Unlike other European nations such as the United Kingdom, France, and even Austria, west Germany did

---

[76] See Associated Press 1995. Also, along the same lines, the French government, for example, planned to use 37.5 billion francs from the French telecommuncations company to lower its 1997 deficit (see IMF Morning Press. 1996.2)

[77] The Economist reported, for example, that "many initial members of the EU monetary union will have used a variety of tricks and gimmicks to qualify for the arrangement, meaning that most of them over the long-run may have to suffer even greater austerity than at present" (Economist, September 21, 1996: 50-51).

[78] West Germany, however, experienced a brief period of a centrally administered economy in which a large number of companies were run by the Allies during 1945-48.

not resort to nationalization as a means of public policy in the years after World War II.[79] Quite the contrary, at a time when some European countries opted for nationalization, Germany initiated its first wave of privatizations. Nevertheless, the public sector increased over time because of an expansion of existing enterprises and the acquisition of new ones by the government.[80] This development is reflected in the fact that the number of companies directly owned by the Federal government (excluding extrabudgetary funds or "Sondervermögen") changed only marginally from 90 in 1962 to 97 in 1970 and 86 in 1980. However, the total number of companies in which the Federal government had ownership directly or indirectly, with stakes of at least 25 percent, increased from 420 in 1962 to a peak of 958 in 1982.[81]

4.4.2   Periods of Privatization

The first wave of privatizations took place in the late 1950s and early 1960s. Three federally owned enterprises were partially privatized: Preussag in 1959, Volkswagen in 1961, and VEBA in 1965. Privatization came, however, to a standstill throughout the late 1960s and 1970s—although no companies were nationalized during this period—and was revived only in the early 1980s after a conservative coalition of Christian Democrats and Free Democrats assumed power. Ever since, the federal government has reduced its holdings of public ownership and in some instances (such as with the remaining shares of VW) fully divested its holdings. However, prior to the most recent push for privatization in the run-up to European Monetary Union (EMU), the government continued to be involved in such varied areas as airports, housing, mining, railways, air travel, and telecommunications. According to the official publication on federally owned enterprises, the government had ownership stakes in more than 400 entities. [82]

As the following tries to establish, the incentives for selling public enterprises have changed over the years and most recently have shifted almost exclusively to meeting fiscal objectives.

4.4.2.1   Privatization 1959-65

Although the political justification for privatization was based on the notion that private ownership is superior to its public counterpart and justified on the grounds of "Ordnungspolitik", the discussion was driven less by efficiency arguments and

---

[79] See Knauss (1993).

[80] According to the Federal Budget Rules (BHO § 65.1), the Federal Government should only establish enterprises or acquire ownership stakes in existing companies if the objectives of the Government cannot be accomplished more efficiently by somebody else. Public enterprises were used to reach objectives ranging from sectoral and regional structural policies to fostering of research and development. See Cox (1993).

[81] See Bundesministerium der Finanzen (various years).

[82] See Bundesministerium der Finanzen (1995).

more by a concept that today is frequently dubbed "peoples' capitalism" and was then frequently referred to as "Volksaktie". The question, for example, of whether widespread ownership undermines efficiency was not even addressed. Furthermore, in most cases the government maintained a controlling share in the company and the sale of shares to the public did not affect employment levels. Although the sale of shares effectively led to a reduction in government ownership, the main objective was to give employees a stake in their own company and to transfer wealth to the general public. With respect to the objective of widespread ownership, the program was quite successful. In the case of the three companies VEBA, VW, and Preussag, the number of buyers amounted to some 2.6 million, 1.5 million and 216 thousand, respectively. Privatization was clearly not seen as a means of increasing budgetary revenues. On the one hand, the objective of achieving widespread ownership could be reached only by imposing limits on the number of shares to be sold to any given investor and by providing special financial incentives that would adversely affect the sales price. On the other hand, in the case of VW, the Government used the proceeds from its sale to create a foundation that would finance scholarships and academic research "Volkswagenstiftung" instead of transferring the funds to the federal budget.[83]

4.4.2.2   Privatization 1984-1994

Just like during the first period of privatization, budgetary considerations were secondary during this period. This statement can be substantiated by analyzing both the total amount of receipts generated during the period and the usage of the funds. The Federal Government received some 13 billion DM during the 10-year period, that is, on average only 1.3 billion a year. Furthermore, 3.3 billion DM of the 13 billion were used to capitalize foundations rather than for budgetary purposes. For example, in the case of the divestiture of the mining and steel company Salzgitter AG, the receipts of 2.5 billion DM were used to set up a foundation that would advise and finance environmental projects.[84] If fiscal considerations were not the prime motive, the question arises whether the government actually privatized to increase efficiency. Certainly, the concept of less government was more in line with the platform and the constituency of the conservative government coalition that first took office in 1982 than with the former more left wing coalition between Social Democrats and Free Democrats. The political success of the British privatization program under Margaret Thatcher probably supported the conviction of the conservative government coalition to pursue a similar strategy, especially since in both countries privatization was seen as a vehicle for spreading ownership widely

---

[83] Prior to the divesture, the Government held 80 percent of the shares of VW. The remaining 20 percent are in the hands of the state of Lower Saxony. Since the Federal Government sold only 60 percent, it continued to hold 20 percent in the company. But even in the case of the remaining 20 percent, the government transferred a large portion of the dividend payments to the foundation instead of using them for budgetary purposes.

[84] See Knaus. 1993. The remaining 800 billion DM from the sale of the 20 percent federally owned Volkswagen shares were transferred to the "Volkswagenstiftung".

and creating a political base that would reward the government for the creation of a new class of small investors in the next election. [85]

4.4.2.3   The current wave of privatization and the role of EMU

While prior to 1994, privatization was not driven by fiscal considerations, this changed dramatically in the run-up to EMU. As one of the key architects of the Maastricht criteria, the German government under Chancellor Kohl had committed itself publicly to meeting both the 3 percent deficit target and the public debt ceiling of 60 percent of GDP. Furthermore, Germany had been among the strongest advocates for a strict interpretation of the criteria in order to convince the skeptical public of the future stability of the common European currency. Meeting the criteria became paramount and a failure to do so would have resulted in a substantial political liability for the conservative coalition government, especially since Chancellor Kohl's personal credibility was at stake.

In line with many governments across the world, the official rhetoric emphasized efficiency arguments as the main rationale for the privatization program. The concept of a leaner government was certainly more in line with the political platforms of both coalition partners, the conservative Christian Democrats (CDU/CSU) and the fiscally conservative liberal Free Democrats (FDP), than with the more socially oriented opposition parties. The then-Minister of Finance Waigel rejected outright the notion that privatization would serve budgetary purposes. In a speech given to CEO's of enterprises formerly owned by the Federal Government, he argued that

... privatization is for us an investment as a foundation for economic competition, efficiency, innovation and economic adjustment of the German economy. We do not use this policy [privatization] as an instrument to improve the position of the budget. Overall economic efficiency considerations are more important to us than short term improvements in revenues" (Waigel, 1995: 16).

Despite the vehement denial by Waigel, Ministry of Finance officials responsible for privatization asserted that budgetary purposes had become the main driving forces for privatization, in clear contrast to earlier periods.[86]

According to deficit calculations based on the European System of National Accounts, privatization receipts were in principle not applicable toward meeting the deficit ceiling. Therefore, the objective of privatization was to lower the debt-to-GDP ratio. As argued before, such an asset swap should be largely without major macroeconomic impacts in the short run, especially if the receipts from privatization are relatively small compared to the stock of outstanding public debt. Therefore, the government's incentives to push for privatization to reduce the debt stock should be negligible. However, with a political commitment by the government and the fact that Germany's debt-to-GDP ratio was slightly higher then the benchmark of 60 percent, the emphasis of the argument changes. The fact that

---

[85] See Waigel (1995).

[86] Based on a discussion with Ministry of Finance officials July 12, 1996.

policymakers directed privatization toward that end was also expressed by the German Anti-Trust Commission in its 1996 Annual Report, which states in its section on privatization that

... fiscal policy arguments to reduce the burden of the public budgets have gained importance. The stock of debt of the general government (federal, state and local budgets as well as extrabudgetary funds) have passed the limit of 60 percent of GDP. At present, Germany is hence disqualified to participate in the European Monetary Union. A substantial reduction of public debt could be reached through a determined privatization strategy. The German Anti-Trust Commission has estimated the total privatization potential for the entire public sector to amount to billions of DM in the three digit level (Monopolkommission, 1996: 56).

Besides an immediate reduction in government debt, privatization would also lead to a reduction in interest payments, lowering the budget deficit. The Anti-Trust Commission assumed that the interest savings would outweigh the loss in budgetary revenues the government would receive from these public enterprises. The willingness of the government to apply whatever means necessary to reach the targets became publicly apparent when it considered reevaluating gold reserves at the German Bundesbank. While massive public outcry and strong resistance from the Bundesbank ultimately prevented the government from proceeding with its reevaluation efforts, the government engaged in numerous other activities to meet the criteria.

The year 1997 was politically especially important since the Kohl administration was facing reelection in 1998 and the fiscal outcome for 1997 would determine which countries would join the first wave of EMU members. At the same time, the prospects for meeting the deficit and debt criteria in 1997 appeared to be remote. Based on government fiscal projections in 1996, the public sector deficit was estimated to be 3.8 percent of GDP (DIW, 1998). The extent to which privatization was pushed in 1997 becomes apparent from figure 4.3. Although privatization receipts had almost continuously increased in the years prior to EMU, receipts peaked in 1997. Furthermore, even though Eurostat had ruled against the counting of privatization receipts toward the deficit target, the German government was able to effectively reduce the deficit by some 2 billion Deutschmark by selling real estate of the German Railway Company to a public entity (Treuhandanstalt) that was not considered to be part of the public sector as well, as through the receipt of oil revenues worth 0.5 billion Deutschmark. The government's attempt to reach the 3 percent deficit target resulted not only in a massive push for privatization but also in other one-time adjustment measures and the temporary postponement of expenditures.[87] According to DIW (1998), 50 percent of the deficit reduction

---

[87] Since the Maastricht criteria apply to the concept of general government but only the Federal Government politically committed to meeting the deficit criteria, the Federal Government started to exert more pressure on the lower levels of government. The potential for privatization receipts on the non-federal levels is quite substantial since these levels of government own large quantities of assets ranging from public utilities, waste disposal, and broadcasting institutions, to insurance companies and banks; the latter account for almost half of all German banking transactions (Brand and Schmitz, 1996)[87]. See Deutsche Bank Research (1994) for a discussion of privatization on the local level.

Figure 4.3. Germany: Privatization Receipts 1/

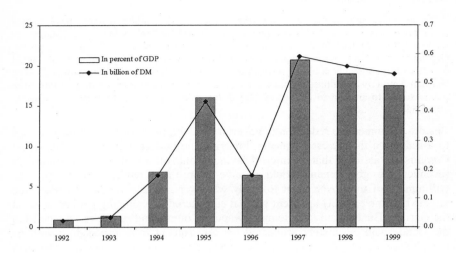

Sources: Bundesministerium der Finanzen (1999); DIW (1998); IMF (1999.1).

1/GDP for the years 1998 and 1999 are estimated. The privatization receipts for 1998 and 1999 are
exlusive of state and local government. Privatization receipts for 1999 are based on budget
projections.

resulted from one-time measures (including the sale of assets). While smaller in
magnitude—and analogous to many developing countries that use privatization
receipts as a means of financing—the German government's effort in reducing the
fiscal deficit to meet the Maastricht criteria were the result of accounting illusions,
leaving the real adjustment to future years.

4.5   Summary

The worldwide wave of privatization is to a large extent driven by fiscal
considerations. As a result of the change in paradigm that has made privatization an
acceptable tool of public policy, governments have discovered an additional source
of financing which has effectively loosened the public sector's one period budget
constraint. Although in many respects the sale of assets is similar to bond financing,
it is not equally scrutinized by the public. The financing of deficits through the
issue of debt instruments is usually watched closely by both the public and financial
markets. The public's assessment of privatization is clouded by the fact that the
fiscal implications of privatization are less transparent than those of other means of

financing. Standard measures of the fiscal stance, such as the public sector deficit and debt stocks, remain either unaffected as a result of privatization or—as in the case where privatization receipts are treated as a revenue equivalent[88]—tend to signal an improvement. This allows policymakers faced with hard budget constraints to resort to asset sales as a quick fix for short-term cash flow problems and to avoid unpopular measures such as real spending cuts. While the fiscal implications of privatization are likely to go unnoticed, policymakers often cannot be held accountable for promised improvements in economic efficiency. Whether improvements in efficiency do indeed materialize will be known only in the medium to long term and most likely not until after the term of the administration that advocated privatization has been completed.

The attractiveness of privatization receipts as an additional source of financing becomes apparent when examining the size of flows that governments received over the past ten years. In some instances such receipts exceeded 4 percent of GDP in a given year. As in the case of developing countries and transition economies that are potentially faced with real financing constraints, industrialized countries are equally inclined to privatize for fiscal reasons, however, largely because of either institutional constraints or for purely political considerations. The German case demonstrates how EMU and the Maastricht criteria encouraged the government to push for privatization. By doing so, the government signaled to the public and financial markets an improvement of the fiscal stance, when in fact much of the improvement consisted of one-time receipts and measures, leaving the intertemporal budget constraint largely unaffected. The use of privatization receipts for such purposes runs the risk of allowing governments to postpone potentially necessary adjustments to future years. To avoid the misuse of privatization for fiscal reasons, privatization receipts should not lower the publicly visible deficit and be treated as financing. Furthermore, the adoption of intergenerational accounting would make the fiscal implications of privatization more transparent.

---

[88] The same occurs when privatization is treated as an expenditure-reducing item.

5 Macroeconomic Considerations of Privatization

While fiscal motives are probably the most important driving force behind large-scale privatization programs in non-former socialist economies, other macroeconomic considerations might also play a role in the decision-making process of policymakers to pursue the divestment of public assets. The following section will analyze monetary, balance-of-payments and employment considerations of privatization.

5.1 Monetary aggregates and inflation

Large privatization programs are likely to have an impact on the price level and monetary aggregates, and may also be used actively as an instrument of monetary policy. Increases in efficiency in the context of a competitive economy should be associated with a fall in prices, assuming that both aggregate demand and monetary policy are unchanged in the aftermath of privatization. Whether privatization affects monetary aggregates and hence inflation depends on a number of factors. In addition to the size of the privatization program, these include the government's use of the receipts, the central bank's monetary policy, the foreign exchange regime, and to whom (foreign or domestic residents) the assets are sold. The following section briefly describes the potential impact of privatization on money and inflation.[89]

In the simplest case, the government does not use the receipts from assets sold domestically to increase government spending, but rather deposits them at the central bank. This leads to a reduction in government liabilities with the central bank. Assuming credit to the private sector and the change in net foreign assets are unaffected, the reduction in net credit to the government results in a reduction in both base money and the money supply. In such a scenario, privatization is similar to an open market operation by the central bank. In line with portfolio selection theory, interest rates would tend to rise in order to entice the private sector to reduce

---

[89] See also Mackenzie (1997) for a discussion about the monetary implications of privatization.

its holdings of money or quasi-money in exchange for less liquid assets. The final impact on interest rates and aggregate demand depends on the openness of the economy as well as the exchange rate system.

Under a flexible exchange rate system, the tendency for interest rates to rise would be associated with a capital inflow and an appreciation of both the nominal and real exchange rates. Since net exports fall as a result of this appreciation, privatization is associated with a reduction in aggregate demand. Under a fixed exchange rate system, the reduction in net credit to the government would be offset by an increase in net international reserves, leaving both interest rates and the money supply unchanged. The latter, of course, requires that inflationary expectations are unaffected. Under either type of exchange rate system, if the government opted to reduce the domestic debt stock of the public sector instead of depositing the divestment proceeds at the central bank, both the money supply and interest rates would remain unchanged.

From a monetary management point of view, the large size of the privatization receipts requires that the sale of assets is taken into consideration in developing a monetary program. Otherwise, neglecting the potential impact of privatization on monetary aggregates could have adverse implications. However, given the difficulties in timing the sale of assets, privatization is not an adequate instrument of discretionary monetary policy. Instead, governments that are guided by short-term political considerations might find it convenient to use privatization as a monetary instrument in the fight against inflation. Persistent high levels of inflation or even hyperinflation are often caused by fiscal imbalances, which implies, that a successful fight against inflation would require fiscal consolidation. As indicated in the modeling exercise, if privatization receipts can be used to replace bank financing and the associated increase in the money supply, the government can reduce inflation temporarily while avoiding such fiscal consolidation.

Such an undertaking would, from a political point of view, kill two birds with one stone. It would allow a reduction in the inflation rate without the corresponding fiscal adjustment. Furthermore, given that privatization is often viewed by the public as an indication of economic adjustment, the announcement of a sale of assets can lead to a change in inflationary expectations even in the absence of a fiscal adjustment. In a world of rational expectations the latter would, of course, require that people are unaware of the use of privatization funds, for example, because of high information costs. Given that the treatment of privatization receipts is often not transparent, it can reasonably be assumed that information costs are extremely high.

Looking, for example, at the case of Argentina, Abdala (1994) establishes that privatization resulted in an improvement in government finances and calculates the impact on inflation. In order to do so, he establishes a counter-factual scenario demonstrating by how much more the government would have had to rely on seigniorage to finance a given level of expenditure without the receipts from privatization.[90] On the basis of an estimated money demand function he then calculates the impact on inflation. The study includes only the sales receipts from the divestment of one public enterprise, the public telephone company ENTEL, which generated cash receipts of U.S. dollar 214 million in the month of October 1990. Without the sale, the estimated growth rate of money would have been 12.1 percent instead of 8.2 percent for the month. Furthermore, inflation would have been 5.6 percent higher had the government opted not to sell the company. The availability of numerous additional large public enterprises, including the public oil company YPF, the national airline Aerolineas Argentinas, and electricity and water companies, allowed the government in subsequent periods to replace seigniorage with sales receipts.

The availability of public assets also helped the Argentinean government introduce a currency board through the so-called Convertibility Plan. Under this self-imposed straight jacket, the government effectively limited its ability to rely on seigniorage, which in earlier periods had provided 3 to 7 percent of government financing. While the political support for a permanent reduction in inflation was extremely high as a result of the painful experiences of earlier hyperinflations, the availability of large privatization receipts allowed the government to reduce inflation while pursuing relatively lax fiscal policies. Without these privatization receipts, fiscal policy would have had to be more draconian, and political support for the anti-inflationary effort would probably have been lower. The use of receipts from divestment gave the Argentine government some breathing space to implement structural reforms necessary to assure the viability of the currency board. However, while the use of privatization receipts can lower inflation temporarily, it bears the risk that short-sighted governments fail to improve the structure of the economy. This could lead not only to a recurrence of previously experienced high rates of inflation but also to substantial welfare costs if arrangements such as a currency board ultimately become unsustainable.[91]

So far the focus has been on the domestic sale of assets and how this affects monetary aggregates and inflation. However, governments might instead opt to sell assets abroad. In particular, countries that are faced with external financing constraints or balances-of-payments crises might be inclined to offer assets to foreign investors. The monetary implications depend, of course, on the choice of the exchange rate system. In the case of a fixed exchange rate system, the inflow of additional capital as a result of privatization will put upward pressure on the nominal exchange rate, forcing the central bank to intervene. In the absence of sterilized intervention, the money supply would increase and large-scale privatization could lead to a surge in inflation. In the case of a flexible exchange rate system, the money supply would not be affected by the increase in capital flows as a result of privatization. However, as a result of the appreciation of both

---

[90] In addition, he calculates the welfare implications of lower inflation rates as a result of privatization.

[91] For currency board issues and experiences see Baliño and Enoch (1997) and Ghosh, Gulde and Wolf (1998).

the nominal and real exchange rates, aggregate demand might be affected adversely in the short term.

5.1.1   Capital inflows

Prior to the East Asian financial crisis that led to the drying up of capital flows to almost all emerging markets, most developing countries and transition economies had experienced substantial surges in capital inflows during the 1990s. As Figure 5.1 shows, private capital flows increased by some 300 percent between 1990 and 1996. As Calvo, Leiderman and Reinhard (1993) point out the surge in capital flows can be attributed to a number of external factors such as declining world interest rates and the rise of large institutional investors with a desire to diversify portfolios. At the same time, capital inflows reflected the fact that international investors had regained confidence in the ability of governments in emerging markets to implement policies that would assure macroeconomic stability and improved growth prospects. In this context, the very fact that countries had started to privatize was interpreted as an indicator of the new policy direction in these countries. However, besides the indirect effect of privatization on capital flows— namely as a signal of the government's reform effort and in conjunction with other reform measures such as economic liberalization and deregulation—the sale of existing public assets to foreign investors contributed directly to the increased inflow in capital. This is partly reflected in rising foreign direct investments as a share of total private capital flows.[92]

The renewed access of developing countries and transition economies in the 1990s to world savings implied the potential for higher growth. At the same time, the size of the flows also posed substantial challenges in terms of macroeconomic management. These challenges were often exacerbated if governments had adopted a fixed exchange rate system in order to break inflationary expectations after periods of high inflation.[93] Besides the fact that the introduction of an exchange rate-based stabilization anchor often contributes itself to the surge in capital flows,

---

[92] The tendency for governments to allow foreign participation was not only limited to emerging markets but could also be found in industrialized countries. In the case of equity issues in OECD countries, foreign participation amounted to almost 50 percent in 1995 compared to 34 percent and 33 percent in 1994 and 1995 respectively (see OECD, 1996).

[93] The advantage of an exchange rate-based stabilization anchor is usually associated with the fact that it reflects a strong commitment on part of the authorities. If the peg is considered credible, people are likely to change their expectations more quickly affecting the setting of wages, prices, and today's interest rates. It is especially advantageous if, after periods of hyperinflation and currency substitution, money demand is difficult to estimate. Shocks in the demand for money are more easily absorbed by endogenous responses in the money supply and hence have smaller effects on output under a fixed exchange rate regime. In contrast, with fixed monetary targets, money demand shocks are likely to have large output effects or, if not observed, undermine the very anchor function. Any government trying to cash in on its stabilization effort politically in the short run is likely to apply an exchange rate anchor. On the discussion about stabilization anchors see Fisher (1986), Vegh (1992), and Tornell and Velasco (1994).

Figure 5.1. Private Capital Flows to Emerging Markets
(In billion U.S. dollars)

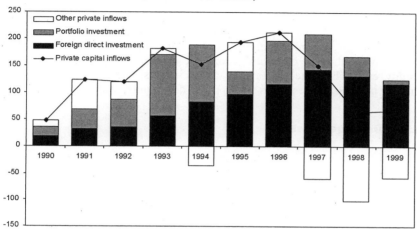

Sources: IMF. 1999. World Economic Outlook—Data Base.

pegging the exchange rate limits the ability of the government to respond. To avoid losing control over the money supply—undermining the government's effort to reduce the growth of money and inflation—the monetary authorities were forced to engage in sterilized interventions. As Calvo points out:

... [the] sterilization of capital inflows has the obvious advantage of keeping money supply under control. However, it will be argued in this note that if the associated open market operation is carried out by expanding the stock of nominal domestic debt, forces may be set in motion that could also jeopardize the credibility—and, hence, sustainability—of the antiinflationary effort (Calvo. 1991: 921).

Governments that have reached high levels of domestic debt might be inclined to use the sale of public assets to domestic investors as a substitute for open market operations. In principle, the implications of using public assets to mop up liquidity should be identical to those of reverse repurchases and the issue of new public debt. In either case the fiscal position of the government deteriorates, leading to an increase in the likelihood of a potential default. The latter would be reflected in a higher risk premium on government debt instruments. Nevertheless, given that the fiscal implications of privatization tend to lack transparency and that the private sector might associate privatization with improvements in economic growth, the impact on the country's perceived default risk might differ in the two cases. The availability of public assets as a substitute for open market operations might be particularly attractive for countries that lack a developed market for government securities. Confronted with sustained surges in capital inflows, the sale of assets could mitigate the monetary implications of such inflows, although the use of privatization for such an end is likely to be limited due to the difficulties in timing the sale of government assets. The sale of assets would, however, be limited to domestic investors.

The above suggests that privatization can potentially undermine the government's effort to control the money supply and reach its inflation targets if it contributes to a prolonged surge in capital inflows. At the same time, governments could be inclined to use the sale of assets to domestic investors as a means of tightening liquidity, especially if faced with large capital inflows. The use of privatization for monetary policy purposes could also apply to debt equity swaps.

5.1.2   Debt-equity swaps

Before 1982, numerous developing countries in Africa and Latin America had seen their external indebtedness mount. Debt-to-GDP ratios in 15 heavily indebted African and Latin American countries increased from 18.5 percent in 1975 to 45.5 percent in 1985. The heavy reliance of these countries on external savings came to a complete standstill as a result of the debt crisis.[94] Despite several attempts to stabilize their economies in the following years, a large number of countries experienced sustained periods of high inflation and low growth. As part of the so-called Brady Initiative in 1989, a consensus emerged that the level of external debt and the corresponding debt service were unsustainable and demanded flexible and innovative solutions. Foreign commercial banks were encouraged to engage in negotiations about debt and debt service reductions through a number of schemes, especially buy-backs and debt-equity swaps. Debt-equity swaps were particularly popular in Latin America. On the one hand and in a standard case, an international commercial creditor bank holding sovereign debt or publicly guaranteed private sector debt sells its debt for foreign currency on the secondary market. Although the debt is traded at a substantial discount, the creditor bank profits since it increases its liquidity by selling an otherwise non-performing asset. On the other hand, a company that intends to invest in the debtor country purchases the debt on the secondary market at a discount and presents the paper to the monetary authority for redemption in local currency either at or below face value. The local currency is then used to acquire ownership stakes in a local company. Investors are able to reap substantial windfall profits due to an implicit foreign exchange subsidy. The debtor country profits from the transaction since it reduces its foreign debt obligation without depleting its foreign exchange reserves. Furthermore, the initial debt-equity swap can function as a catalyst if the investment of an existing stock of assets by a foreign company leads to additional new investments in the future.

Despite the attractiveness of such swaps for both the investor and the government, debt-equity swaps have drawbacks. Apart from the fact that the government has to bear the cost of an exchange rate subsidy—which is questionable if the foreign investment would take place without the swaps—debt-equity swaps tend to be

---

[94] For a brief overview of debt issues and the debt crisis, see Munla (1992).

inflationary in a fixed exchange rate regime. After all, debt-equity-related capital inflows are equivalent to any other form of foreign capital inflows. To offset the injection of additional liquidity, the government could, of course, issue securities. However, especially in countries with underdeveloped capital markets and a public sector that has a track record of defaulting on its liabilities, the budgetary implications of sterilizing debt-equity swap-related inflows could be substantial, undermining the very reason for using swaps in the first place. Hence, the application of debt-equity swaps is constrained by monetary policy objectives. Some countries, such as Mexico and Chile, had to discontinue their swaps or impose a quota system in order not to jeopardize their inflation targets.[95] Nations that are confronted with the adverse monetary implications of debt-equity swaps could resort to privatization to fend off inflationary pressures. Some countries such as Argentina tied the privatization of assets directly to a reduction in external debt.[96]

5.2   Balance-of-payments crises

Governments often resort to privatization for fiscal reasons and might also use privatization in pursuit of monetary policy targets. Balance-of-payments crises are an additional key determinant of privatization. Evidence for this can be found in the case of the Mexican crisis in 1994, the financial crisis in East Asia in 1997/98, the run on the Russian currency in 1998, and the forced devaluation of the Brazilian currency in 1999.[97] In each case, a sudden change in market sentiment led to reversal of capital flows. For example, in the case of the five East Asian countries (Thailand, Indonesia, Korea, Malaysia, and the Philippines) the Institute for International Finance (1998) estimates that net private capital flows fell from 93 billion U.S. dollars in 1996 to about -12 billion U.S dollars in 1997, a change equivalent to about 11 percent of the five countries' combined GDP. Since all of the above-mentioned countries had relied on either a fixed exchange rate system or a crawling peg prior to the crisis, the reversal in capital flows ultimately forced the countries to abandon their pegs, causing the exchange rate to fall precipitously.

Although the causes of the attacks differed across countries, ranging from "first generation" or macroeconomic-policy-induced crises (e.g. Thailand and Russia), to financial panics (e.g. Mexico and Korea) and financial contagion (e.g. Brazil), policymakers in each country resorted to privatization as one of the key elements in their emergency macroeconomic stabilization program. For example, the Thai program states that:

---

[95] See Asian Finance (1988) and Basile (1990).

[96] For a detailed discussion of the mechanics of the debt-equity swaps in the context of the Argentine privatization process see Markey (1991) and HBS (1992).

[97] For a description of the Mexican crises see Sachs, Tornell , and Velasco (1996) as well as HBS (1996). On the causes of the Brazilian crises see IMF (1999). On the Russian and East Asian crises see IMF (1998.1); Radelet and Sachs (1998) and Kochhar, Loungani and Stone (1998).

Privatization is one of the key medium-term goals of our program. We have completed the preliminary work needed to increase the role of the private sector in energy, public utilities, communications, and transport sectors. We expect to announce firm plans in these areas by June 1998. The majority owned state enterprises which are already corporatized will be the first ones to be privatized. Indeed, we intend to reduce the government's stake in the national airline (currently 93 percent) and Bangchak petroleum company (currently 80 percent) to well below 50 percent by mid-1998, if market conditions permit. We also intend to submit to Parliament by June 1998, the necessary legislation to facilitate the privatization of the state enterprises which are not currently corporatized (Government of Thailand, 1997: 4).

The Thai program also explicitly states that a significant amount of resources will be raised through the sale of assets and that a key objective of the divestment effort is to "attract more nondebt-creating capital inflows" (Government of Thailand, 1997: 3). The same applies to Indonesia, where privatization is a key component of the adjustment program. For the fiscal year 1999 alone, the government intends to raise some 1.5 billion U.S. dollars or 1 percent of GDP in privatization receipts. [98]

The same push for privatization took place in Brazil. The Brazilian adjustment program states that:

The government intends to accelerate and further broaden the scope of its privatization program—already one of the most ambitious in the world. In 1999 it intends to complete the privatization of federal electricity generation companies, and in 2000 it will begin the privatization of the electricity transmission network. At the state level, most remaining state-owned electricity distribution companies are expected to be privatized in 1999. ... Total receipts from privatization are projected at around R$27.8 billion (nearly 2.8 percent of GDP) (of which R$24.2 billion at the federal level) in 1999 and at R$22.5 billion over the period 2000-2001 (Government of Brazil, 1999).

The intended objective of the privatization programs, combined with other measures of macroeconomic adjustment, is to signal to international financial markets the governments' commitment to improving the structure of the economy by relying more on market forces and less on government intervention. At the same time, the willingness of governments to sell assets to foreigners and to allow foreigners to acquire majority ownership in enterprises and financial institutions that had previously been considered "off limits" can be seen as an effort by the governments to alleviate the crisis by using privatization as a form of "exceptional financing". This attempt is being made even in the face of depressed asset prices and the likelihood that domestic investors will be more reluctant to enter the bidding process as a result of the domestic recession.

The sale of assets to foreign investors as a means of attracting a direct inflow (or reducing the outflow) of foreign capital is, of course, not necessarily incompatible with the objective of long-run improvements in efficiency. Some of the more recent economic programs supported by international financial institutions such as the IMF and the World Bank include, for example, provisions to assure that balance-of-payments-induced privatizations are likely to lead to improvements in efficiency. Such programs usually stipulate that the sale of assets has to be transparent and rely

---

[98] See Government of Indonesia (1999). The sale of public entities has also been an important component of the Korean economic program. See Government of Korea (1999).

on market-based privatization strategies.[99] However, it is the incentive structure that policymakers face that make them vulnerable to exploiting privatization to attract capital inflows and to minimize the short-term cost of the crises even at the cost of long-term economic welfare. For example, whereas under normal circumstances policymakers would tend to have a selection bias toward domestic investors for domestic political reasons (for example, to please particular interest groups or engage in insider deals), during a balance-of-payments crisis the bias would most likely be toward foreign investors. Biases in either direction lead to a suboptimal allocation of resources.

When privatization is driven by currency crises, governments may be tempted to grant specific concessions, to restrict competition in the privatized sectors of the economy, and to favor non-transparent private negotiations instead of public auctions and bidding processes. Furthermore, governments that engage in privatization for balance-of-payments reasons might fail to establish regulatory agencies in order to avoid market restrictions in the privatized industries. If external conditions require the establishment of such agencies, governments might fail to provide adequate resources and staffing. In the case of the privatization of financial institutions, governments might fail to set up supervisory agencies (see the case study on Jamaica). Also, given that the government's incentive is to divest its assets as soon as possible, the danger of adverse selection arises.

The very fact that large-scale privatization is the result of a balance-of-payments crisis warrants caution. With the exception of countries that are in distress as a result of a financial panic or contagion rather than poor economic management, a balance-of-payments crisis by itself suggests that policymakers neglected to address macroeconomic imbalances or an overvaluation of the currency in the first place, or in a less benign case directly contributed to the crisis. From a welfare point of view an early but orderly adjustment would have been superior to a forced adjustment by market forces, which is often associated with large exchange rate overshooting, severe recession, high rates of unemployment and economic hardship. Failure to make an early adjustment may reflect shortsightedness or the desire not to alienate key constituencies. Policymakers that reveal such preferences by not implementing adjustment efforts early on are likely to use privatization in a manner that would minimize the short-term effects of the crisis even at the expense of long-term improvements in efficiency and growth. Similar short-term behavior has often been demonstrated by governments that addressed fiscal crises by cutting expenditure and raising taxes, thus favoring measures that addressed the government's cash-flow position and macroeconomic balances in the short term while undermining the long-run growth potential of the economy. In such cases, policymakers frequently opt to cut capital expenditure instead of current expenditure, given that the political resistance would be higher in the case of the latter. At the same time, tax increases

---

[99] For example, the Indonesian economic program states that: "A clear framework will be established for the management and privatization (either through share flotation or negotiated enterprise sale) of government assets by the time of the first review, including: (i) criteria for determining whether enterprises should be closed, restructured or fully privatized, and (ii) a transparent sales process that maximizes the return to government from sales and treats all bidders equally". (Government of Indonesia. 1997: 10).

are designed to produce the highest growth in revenues in the short term. In either instance this behavior undermines the growth potential of the economy. In the case of cuts in capital expenditure the government undermines the growth potential directly; in case of tax increases that are imposed on factors of labor and capital instead of consumption, the economy is adversely affected through distortions.

5.3   Employment considerations of privatization

Governments that decide to go ahead with privatization are confronted with the problem of unemployment given the tendency of public enterprises to suffer from over-employment. While overstaffing might be a function of poor management and inadequate control, public enterprises are frequently charged by governments with pursuing non-commercial objectives that are at odds with profit maximization. One of these functions is to serve as "an employer of last resort". Despite the fact that the level of over-employment in public enterprises varies across countries, industries, and firms, it is generally believed that the potential for improvements in labor productivity as a result of privatization is large.

The evidence that public enterprises suffer from overstaffing is revealed in numerous case studies. Donahue (1989), for example, indicates that employment per unit of output is higher for services provided by public municipalities in the United States than for those provided by their private counterparts. In the case of Japan, Watanabe (1994) calculates that 22 percent of the Japanese National Railway Company could be made redundant as a result of privatization.[100] Banerji and Sabot (1994) indicate that overemployment in Turkish and Indian public enterprises amounts to almost 35 percent. In some of these cases, it is believed that overstaffing in public enterprises could reach 50 percent or more.[101] According to a World Bank study by Kikeri (1998), overstaffing is most prevalent in public enterprises that operate in protected markets and that rely heavily on government subsidies, such as large steel companies.

When such entities are transferred to the private sector, profit-maximizing private owners that are not constrained in terms of employment levels are likely to reduce the workforce to bring real wages in line with the marginal product of labor.

5.3.1   Efficiency of labor markets

Whether and to what degree the reduction in employment results in open unemployment and whether the increase is temporary or long-term will depend partly on a number of factors. In the neoclassical world, freed resources are re-

---

[100] The Japanese Water Company employed some 276 thousand people prior to privatization.

[101] Kikeri (1998) mentions that 40-50 percent of the 120 thousand employees of public enterprises could be made redundant. Another study by the World Bank (1994) indicates that 50 percent of the Argentine railway company (Renfe) could be made redudant.

employed in other sectors of the economy, leading to higher levels of income and an improvement in the standard of living of the population.

Initially, the degree to which the new private owners will lay off surplus workers will depend on the willingness of the employees to accept real wage cuts. Indeed, a number of studies show that employees faced with the threat of unemployment are willing to accept substantial paycuts.

However, given the degree of overstaffing in many public enterprises, downward flexibility in real wages is not likely to be sufficient to assure continued employment. Since labor markets are imperfect and the creation of new jobs is likely to proceed slowly, to occur in other regions of the country, or to require skills that are not readily available, unemployment increases in the short-term. In addition to temporary unemployment increases, the equilibrium long-run unemployment rate might rise as well.

If privatization is associated with the development of a more dynamic private sector, frictional unemployment is likely to increase permanently. Assuming that the time for unemployed people to find a job is unchanged, a more dynamic economy would be equivalent to a higher search rate at any given point in time. In addition, structural unemployment might increase. The potential for a more permanent increase in the unemployment rate occurs if labor markets are inefficient. In particular, it will depend on the unemployment compensation system; the wage bargaining system; and regulations concerning the procedures for dismissal, length of the workweek, and part-time work.

Countries in which the government was a dominant player in terms of both ownership and intervention are also likely to have highly regulated labor markets. Hence, a reduction in government ownership without the simultaneous liberalization of the labor market will lead to increases not only in temporary but also permanent unemployment. Any future increases in efficiency are likely to lead to increases in real wages rather than employment levels.

Policymakers that engage in privatization for short-term objectives might not adequately address labor market reform. Inconsistencies of government policies toward improving the structure of the economy can be found in both industrialized countries and emerging economies. While governments reduced the size of the private sector through privatization—potentially because of short-term reasons—little attention had been given to reforming the labor market. For example, Spain has a highly regulated labor market but engaged in large-scale privatization. The failure to liberalize the labor market in tandem with privatization has probably contributed to the increase in structural unemployment over the past decade to almost 20 percent. [102] The failure to accompany a massive privatization program with a reform of the labor market can also be found in Argentina, where unemployment rates have increased from 5.9 percent at the beginning of the privatization program in 1988 to 16.3 percent in 1996.

---

[102] On the strictness of labor market regulation see IMF (1999), OECD (1994), and OECD (1993).

The fact that labor market issues have been neglected in the current wave of privatization and economic reform prompted the World Bank to address these issues in its 1995 World Development Report by drawing up a list of policies to foster employment restructuring. Among the most important ones are recommendations to facilitate labor mobility, increase wage flexibility, and reduce disincentives to changing jobs. Since governments that try to address such issues will encounter severe opposition by strong interest groups, it is not surprising that most governments have engaged in privatization without adequately addressing labor market issues. However, this political disincentive to reform must be weighed against the negative political consequences of higher unemployment as a result of privatization. As indicated above, by neglecting to reform labor markets, unemployment should go up in the aftermath of privatization, especially in countries that engage in a large transfer of ownership over a short period of time. Without measures to alleviate the adverse impact of privatization on employment, a drastic increase in the unemployment rate would politically be extremely costly for governments.

In addition to potentially affecting structural unemployment, privatization can also lead to an increase in cyclical unemployment. If privatization leads to a large displacements of the workforce, divestment is likely to be associated with an adverse impact on aggregate demand as a result of the loss in income, further exacerbating the implications for employment. However, a potentially mitigating factor could be that investment demand rises in the aftermath of a privatization if private investors expect the economy to improve in the medium term.

5.3.2   Privatization and unemployment

A cursory view of unemployment rates and privatization illustrates that in most countries the beginning of large divestment programs—defined as programs that yield at least 0.5 percent of GDP in gross receipts—coincides with an increase in the unemployment rate in the same year.[103] Figure 5.2 shows unemployment rates in the year the privatization program began (t) as well as the preceding (t-1) and following (t+1) years. However, an analysis of privatization and aggregate unemployment is clouded by a number of factors. First, privatization might be associated with other economic reform measures, such as macroeconomic

---

[103] Although the use of gross receipts from privatization represents a standardized measure that can be applied across countries, it has a number of caveats. A country could transfer ownership from the public to the private sector without generating any or only a small amount of receipts. This was exemplified in many former socialist economies that chose large-scale voucher privatization. Also, while the sales of capital-intensive companies is often associated with large sales receipts, it often has little impact on employment. Furthermore, the use of gross receipts to determine the beginning of a large-scale privatization program does not take into account expenditures that the government might incur or the assumption of debt by the government. Nevertheless, the dates that are being identified on the basis of gross-privatization receipts are broadly in line with other indicators that could have been applied to determine the beginning of a large-scale privatization program.

Figure 5.2. Privatization and Unemployment Rates

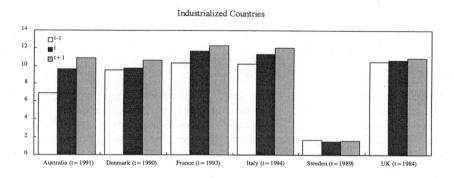

Industrialized Countries

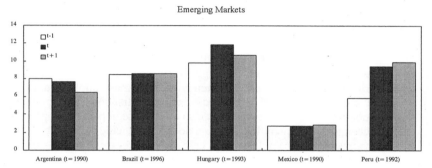

Emerging Markets

Sources: IMF. International Financial Statistics; IMF. World Economic Outlook.

stabilization and trade liberalization, that may have adverse impacts on the level of employment in the short term. Second, it is unclear whether privatization precedes unemployment or whether an economic downturn causes governments to divest in order to raise funds to address rising government deficits and avoid a further contraction of the economy due to required expenditure cuts. Furthermore—as will be discussed below—the measured rates of unemployment in the aftermath of privatization can either over- or understate the real impact on employment.

On the sectoral and company level, a number of studies suggest that privatization is associated with a substantial reduction in the workforce. Bhaskar and Khan (1995) show, for example, how privatization affected employment in Bangladesh's key export industry. Over a four-year period in the early 1980s, Bangladesh transferred half of its textile mills to their former owners, while the other half remained in the hands of the government. Unlike most other privatizations, the selection process was not based on the performance of the companies but on whether they had been owned by Bengalis or West Pakistanis at the time of nationalization. Since the government set minimum wages that affected both the private and the public sector and were considered to be rather excessive, the potential for downward wage adjustments was limited and any changes by the new private owners would hence have employment impacts. In line with the discussion above, the government limited the employment impacts by imposing a one-year ban on dismissals. Bhaskar and Khan show that after five years the workforce had been reduced by a total of about 32 percent. In the case of Argentina, Shaikh (1996) shows that after the privatization of five large public enterprises, the workforce in these firms was reduced by 30 percent. Overall, employment in privatized companies fell from almost 225 thousand to 111 thousand.

However, while these studies suggest that the privatization of public enterprises can lead to substantial retrenchment on the company level, no inferences can be made about the overall level of unemployment. The case of Argentina is especially telling since—at least at the beginning of the privatization process—only a certain portion of the retrenched workers contributed to an increase in the measured unemployment rate, given that the government transferred some of the workers to other government agencies and encouraged early retirements.[104]

When, whether and to what degree measured unemployment rises as a result of privatization depends on a number of factors.

- The timing of the layoffs. Kikeri (1998) shows that in a number of cases governments reduce the level of employment prior to privatization. Such restructuring prior to privatization is often intended to make public entities more attractive and to increase the proceeds from privatization. While the pre-privatization retrenchment exercise has also an adverse impact on employment levels, a change in the unemployment rate does not coincide with the beginning of the privatization program. Instead, in cases where the workforce was reduced before privatization, the actual sale of enterprises to the private sector might lead to an increase in employment and a reduction in the unemployment rate.

- The impact on the labor force participation rate. If workers of public enterprises are made redundant, such layoffs might result in a decrease in the labor force participation rate. Evidence for this can be found in transition economies where public enterprise workers, especially female workers, left the labor force altogether after privatization.[105]

- The implementation of early retirement plans. In some cases governments have addressed the issue of over-employment by allowing workers to take early retirement. Transel (1996), for example, points out that 70 percent of the workers that were dismissed in the context of the privatization of the Turkish cement industry opted to retire after dismissal, thereby leaving the labor market altogether.

---

[104] See Kikeri (1998). For privatization in Japan and the Japanese railway company see Köster (1998).

[105] See, for example, Klaasen (1994).

- The creation of temporary unemployment programs. The creation of temporary retraining programs for retrenched employees also implies that they are not counted as unemployed.

Governments that receive their political support from labor or that are faced with strong unions have an incentive to avoid increases in unemployment as a result of privatization. In principle it can be assumed that politicians who depend on voters for their survival have an incentive to minimize any adverse impact of privatization on employment, to buy out the respective interest groups through generous transfer payments, and to manage any dismissals in such a manner that they encounter little public resistance. Any measure, for example, that avoids raising the measured unemployment rate would fall into this category. The latter takes place when governments provide early retirement packages or offer retraining programs. In addition, governments might opt to get employment commitments from private investors.

5.3.3   Employment commitments

Governments that try to assure that privatization is not immediately associated with an increase in unemployment are inclined to limit the ability of private investors to dismiss workers freely. At the time of the purchase of the company, the new investors commit themselves either implicitly or even explicitly through a contractual arrangement to maintaining a certain—often pre-privatization—employment level for a specified period. While such agreements avoid the often politically costly increase in unemployment, they undermine the very rationale for privatization, that is, a reallocation of resources toward their most productive use. Furthermore, they directly transfer income from the general taxpayer to those that profit from the employment guarantee. This transfer occurs since private investors will discount the additional cost by lowering their bidding prices. The true fiscal costs of such employment commitments are, of course, non-transparent and hence there will be little political opposition. While the benefits are tangible for those that profit from such schemes, taxpayers who in the first place have only a marginal stake in providing the subsidy are faced with large information costs.

One of the most extreme cases of "hidden" subsidies to public enterprise workers on a massive scale occurred in the process of privatizing firms in the former East Germany. Potential investors were asked explicitly by the government to quote, in addition to the sales price and the amount of future investment, the level of employment to which they would be willing to commit. In weighing the three components—price, amount of future investments, and employment commitment—the German government put the most weight on the latter, which often implied "giving the company away" at a nominal sales price of one deutschmark.[106] A number of case studies show that employment guarantees are a frequent feature of

---

[106] For an overview of privatization in East Germany including the criteria for selecting privatization bids see Brücker (1995). See also Bös and Kayser (1995).

privatization programs around the globe and can be found in countries such as Mexico, Sri Lanka, Bangladesh, and Malaysia.[107]

5.3.4   Severance payments and retrenchment benefits

In cases where governments do not resort to employment guarantees to minimize the political cost of privatization-related unemployment, governments are tempted to limit the adverse political ramifications of unemployment by offering generous transfer payments in the form of retrenchment or severance payments to workers of public enterprises. As in the case of employment guarantees, these payments frequently are not transparent and not reflected in budgetary outlays even though they are likely to have a large impact on the net wealth position of the government.

Such payments could be justified if employees of public enterprises acquired rights during their tenure that are lost as a result of privatization. Such rights include, inter alia, lifetime employment guarantees, pension rights, and an implicit form of unemployment insurance.[108] Unless the government wants to breach its legal obligations and bear the cost of losing its credibility, retrenchment or severance benefits reflect a buy-out and should be equivalent to the net present value of these rights. Such a buyout would merely convert an implicit liability of the government into an explicit one and could therefore be considered to be fiscally neutral. However, the risk of such buyouts lies in the fact that governments faced with political opposition might be inclined to offer retrenchment benefits and severance payments that exceed those that could be justified based on previously acquired rights. The increase in the liabilities might undermine some of the expected positive aspects of privatization, contributing to higher future tax rates and increasing economic distortions rather than improving economic efficiency.

As table 5.1 and numerous studies show, retrenchment benefits and severance packages have indeed been extremely generous. In many of the countries that have provided large retrenchment benefits and severance packages, lifetime employment was limited to civil servants rather than extending to employees of public enterprises. Social considerations such as alleviating the adverse implications of unemployment for the affected groups do not appear to justify some of the transfer payments. The provision of generous transfer payments in the process of privatization is often facilitated by a lack of transparency. As the following case study on Pakistan shows, receipts from privatization are at times channeled through extrabudgetary funds rather than the government budget. Hence, the use of these funds is not equally scrutinized by Parliament during budget appropriations. Without a public debate, expenditures for retrenchment and severance payments do

---

[107] See Kikeri (1998).

[108] Assuming that unemployment is likely to increase due to the rationalization of privatized enterprises, severance payments can reduce the social hardship associated with the temporary loss of employment and are especially warranted in countries lacking an adequate unemployment insurance system. A large number of developing countries lack any form of unemployment compensation altogether.

Table 5.1. Retrenchment Benefits in Selected Countries

Country	
Algeria	1 month of salary per year of service
Argentina 1/	24 months of salary
Bangladesh 2/	36 months of salary
Brazil 3/	18 months of salary
Central African Republic	40 months of salary plus the employee's accumulated pension fund contribution
Ghana	4 months of basic salary plus 2 months of basic salary per year of service
Guinea	60 months of average basic salary
Laos	Last month of basic salary per year of service plus an additional year and one year of child allowance
Pakistan	For unionized workers: 5 months of basic salary for each year of service; for non-unionized workers: 3 months of basic salary for each year of service
Philippines	1.5 months of salary per year of service

Source: Kikeri (1998); IMF(1995); and Government of Pakistan (1995).

1/ Actual average payment in the case of the privatization of Ferrocarriles Argentinas, Entel, and Somisa.

2/ Actual average payments in the case of the privatization of jute (BJMC).

3/ Actual average payment in the case of railways privatization

not have to compete with other current expenditures. Governments that channel privatization receipts through extrabudgetary funds can use the receipts at their own discretion. Often the supervision or the authorization for the usage of these funds lies solely with the government in power. In many of the countries listed, lifetime employment had not been guaranteed and tended to be more typical for civil servants than for employees of public enterprises. Also, in most of the cases workers were able to maintain their pension rights. For these reasons, the validity of property rights arguments is negligible. It is also clear that in many cases the argument of alleviating the adverse effects of unemployment—that is, retrenchment payments serving the function of a social safety net—cannot be applied. Retrenchment benefits in Guinea, for example, would be equivalent to five years of unemployment compensation. Hence, for all practical purposes, the first two points can be discarded. The question of whether such generous retrenchment packages were necessary because of political constraints is closely related to the discussion of transparency and the institutional set-up.

5.4   Political considerations and retrenchment benefits: the case of Pakistan

As indicated in the section above, improvements in efficiency of privatized enterprises often require a substantial reduction in the work force. It can be assumed that governments have incentives to minimize the adverse political consequences of large layoffs. Besides directly constraining private owners from reducing the workforce, governments can use retrenchment and severance packages to make large transfer payments to those affected by privatization.

In order to quantify the potential magnitude of such transfer payments, the following analyzes in more depth the privatization process in Pakistan. Pakistan serves as a prime example since the government's privatization program was met with severe political opposition from the outset, especially from organized labor. To avoid a political standoff, successive governments have provided extremely generous retrenchment benefits. While the strategy allowed the government to proceed with its privatization program, it poses the risk of increasing the liabilities of the public sector, possibly undermining the economy's growth potential. The case of Pakistan also shows how an institutional set-up that lacks transparency prevents a public debate about the merits of such buy-outs and allows policymakers to commit public resources at the expense of overall economic welfare.

5.4.1   Background

Like many governments in the developing world, Pakistan relied for many years on an inward-looking development and import substitution policy. In the 1970s, the government of Prime Minister Ali Bhutto embarked on a wave of nationalizations that included not only the productive sector but also the banking system and the insurance sector. As a result, the government was directly involved in the production of goods and services in most sectors of the economy except sugar and textiles. At the end of the 1980s, the government controlled 75 corporations either through majority shareholding or through joint ownership with provincial governments and other public corporations. Most of the corporations in turn were holding companies each comprising several individual enterprises. Overall, the government controlled some 177 pubic entities in 1990.[109] In certain sub-sectors such as cement, automobiles, fertilizer, and vegetable oil, the government contributed some 50 percent or more to total output.[110]

---

[109] The number of public enterprises includes also the Water and Power Development Authority and the Pakistan Telecommunication Corporation, which are legally government departments rather than separate public enterprises.

[110] For an overview of the size of the public sector see also Naqvi and Kemal (1991).

Compared to other developing countries, the share of the public sector in total economic activity was not overly large, amounting to about 12 percent in 1991; employment in public enterprises as a percent of the non-agricultural labor force was 3.6 percent (see Table 5.2). However, despite the limited contribution to both employment and total output in the economy, the public sector accounted for more than 50 percent of domestic investments.

Even though the size of the public sector was not particularly large in Pakistan, loss-making public enterprises contributed to a large extent to the poor fiscal performance of the country, with fiscal deficits hovering between 7 and 8 percent during the second half of the 1980s (see Table 5.3). A number of authors argue fiscal considerations supplied the prime motive for Pakistan's move toward privatization.[111] Naqvi and Kemal, for example, state that:

Even more than securing greater allocative and productive efficiency, the urgency to reduce fiscal deficits has been the main driving force to privatize through assets sales. .... The problem of raising enough financial resources has become acute, particularly because of the government's reluctance to raise tax revenues; and because it is more difficult to raise additional resources for financing the deficit (Naqvi and Kemal. 1991: 119).

First attempts to arrest the high fiscal deficits through privatization were made by the administration of Benazir Bhutto of the Pakistan People's Party (PPP) in 1988. However, the government's assumption that it could sell loss-making public enterprises at predetermined minimum prices and without major impacts on employment levels turned out to be erroneous. During the two years the PPP was in office, the government failed to sell a single entity.[112] The PPP was succeeded by the opposition Pakistan Muslim League (PML), which announced that it would make the rationalization and privatization of state enterprises the cornerstone of its economic program. After the establishment of a privatization commission in 1991, 118 public enterprises were identified for privatization and over the next two years the government sold some 67 public entities to the private sector. Even the return to power by Benazir Bhutto and the PPP in 1993 did not lead to a major deviation from the previous privatization strategy, nor did the change of administrations in the following years.[113]

---

[111] Masihuddin states that: "In order to give a boost to the economy major reforms have been introduced since 1988 of which Privatisation is one of the most important components. Th(e) main objective is to reduce the financial burden caused by persistent losses of the public enterprises and to release resources for utilization in social sectors hitherto badly neglected and development of physical and technological infrastructure. It is a fact that a fair quantum of budgetary resources has been used to subsidize the public enterprises." (Masihuddin, 1994: 4); see also Aziz (1996).

[112] The only divestment that took place was the sale of 10 percent of non-voting shares in Pakistan's national airline carrier; see Kirkness and Style (1996) and Naqvi and Kemal (1994).

[113] On the privatization program of the Benazir Bhutto government see Privatisation Commission (1994). On the government's current strategy see Government of Pakistan (1998). Enhanced Structural Adjustment Facility Policy Framework Paper, 1998/99-2001/01. Washington, D.C. (IMF).

Table 5.2. Pakistan: Employment Prior to Privatization

	Local	Provincial	Federal 1/	Total
General Government				
Number (in thousand)	195	1,254	1,158	2,607
Share of total general government				
employees (in percent)	7.5	48.1	44.4	100.0
Share of non-				
agricultural employment (in percent)	1.3	8.3	7.7	17.3
Public Enterprises				
Number (in thousand)	0	101	437	538
Share of total public enterprise				
employees (in percent)	0.0	18.8	81.2	100.0
Share of non-				
agricultural employment (in percent)	0.0	0.7	2.9	3.6
Total public sector employment				
Number (in thousand)	195	1,355	1,595	3,145
Share of total public sector				
employees (in percent)	6.2	43.1	50.7	100.0
Share of non-				
agricultural employment (in percent)	1.3	9.0	10.6	20.9

Source: National Manpower Commission, 1989; Government Sponsored Corporation, 1989-90; and

Civil Servants Census, 1989.

5.4.2   Political opposition to privatization and retrenchment benefits

One of the problems that the respective administrations encountered in Pakistan is strong opposition to privatizing both state-owned enterprises and the financial sector. The opposition came especially from organized labor and strong unions.[114] The political opposition stemmed largely from the fact that overstaffing in the public enterprises was rampant and that privatization would be associated with a dramatic reduction in employment and an increase in unemployment.[115] Given the fact that public enterprises tended to employ educated workers, it was likely that politically active white-collar employees would be affected.[116] In addition, public employees enjoyed numerous fringe benefits such as subsidized housing and medical benefits as well as low-interest loans. Aziz, for example, indicates that "indirect costs per employee were about twice as large as the corresponding costs in the private sector." (Aziz, 1996:32). In response to the government's announcement that it would proceed with privatization, unions effectively blocked potential investors and consultants from entering company premises for evaluation purposes. Furthermore, the different public sector unions created an umbrella organization, the All Pakistan State Enterprises Workers Action Committee (APSEWAC), in order to increase their effectiveness in dealing with the government.[117]

Successive governments, mindful of the political consequences of higher unemployment and the potential for outright strikes, opted to buy out the opposition by offering generous severance packages.[118] A key component of the program and that of later administrations has been to offer extremely large retrenchment benefits—so-called "golden handshakes"—to those who would voluntarily leave the public entity at the time of divestment. While labor laws in Pakistan already stipulate that in the case of a dismissal both private and public sector employers have to pay a gratuity of one month per year of service, the government's buy-out package provides an additional four months of basic salary for each year of service

---

[114] See Kirkness and Style (1996).

[115] Prior to privatization, unemployment rates were relatively low. However, the modest unemployment rates reflect the fact that the country does not have a comprehensive unemployment insurance scheme, forcing able-bodied persons to work. Privatization- related increases in unemployment therefore create social and economic hardship that might not be encountered in countries with an unemployment benefit system. Furthermore, in the case of Pakistan, privatization-related unemployment is exacerbated by a high dependency ratio since about 3 people depend on the income of one wage earner and by the fact that a large percentage of the population is underemployed. See Economic Survey (1994).

[116] Naqvi and Kemal (1994) mention that more than 50 percent of the work force could be made redundant.

[117] See also Aziz (1996).

[118] Initially, the unions had asked for retrenchment benefits that would have amounted to payments of 7 months of wages for each year of service.

Table 5.3. Pakistan: Selected Economic Indicators

	75-79	80-84	85-89	90	91	92	93	94	95	96	97	98
Current account deficit (in percent of GDP)	-5.4	-2.6	-2.8	-3.8	-2.7	-3.7	-7.7	-3.0	-4.0	-7.1	-5.8	-2.9
Fiscal balance (in percent of GDP)	-8.5	-6.1	-8.0	-7.7	-8.5	-8.0	-8.2	-6.0	-5.6	-6.9	-6.5	-5.5
Inflation	10.5	8.4	6.1	9.1	11.6	3.6	9.8	11.3	12.4	10.3	12.5	7.8
Economic growth	5.2	6.3	6.4	4.5	5.5	7.8	1.9	3.9	5.2	4.7	-0.4	5.4
Unemployment rate 1/	n.a.	3.9	3.3	3.1	6.3	5.8	4.8	4.8	4.8	4.8	4.0	3.8

Sources: IMF. World Economic Outlook.

1/ The average for 1980-84 includes only data for 1983 and 1984.

in the case of unionized workers. Non-unionized workers, managerial personal, and workers over 58 years of age are entitled to a voluntary separations scheme equivalent to a total of three months of wages per year of service[119]; non-unionized workers can, however, join the union at any time, allowing them to qualify for the full benefits of five months.[120] In addition to the generous retrenchment package, the government also agreed to request from potential bidders an employment guarantee of one year for those that chose to remain employed and to provide unemployment compensation for up to two years after the employment guarantee expires in case the new owners were to reduce employment further.[121]

5.4.3   Costs and impacts of the buyout of surplus workers

Data from the Privatization Commission (1994) show that more than 55 percent of the workers of enterprises in the initial privatizations availed themselves of the retrenchment benefit package.[122] In some of the industries, such as rice, vegetable ghee and engineering, more than 60 percent of the employees opted for the government's retrenchment program. Seventeen thousand workers were affected by

---

[119] Comprising one month of full wage and 2 months of basic salary for each year of service.

[120] See Kemal (1993).

[121] Also, the privatization program allows for the acquisition of the company by the employees. Employees can use their severance payment in order to purchase the company.

[122] Out of an affected workforce of 17,897 employees, 9,831 opted for the golden handshake.

the first wave of privatization and total outlays for retrenchments amounted to rupees 1.2 billion (43 million U.S. dollars).[123] The evidence from the first wave of privatization suggests that overstaffing amounted to more than 50 percent given that the new owners tended to shed labor even further after the guaranteed employment period expired. Both the agreement between the government and employee representation for the public enterprises (APSEWAC) as well as the actual payments made during the first wave of privatizations set a precedent for future privatizations. In effect—and as long as the country follows through with its privatization objectives—the government has implicitly assumed additional liabilities.

While the adverse fiscal implications of the initial retrenchment packages were relatively small and are not likely to have broader macroeconomic implications, the government committed itself to providing similar retrenchment benefits in future privatizations. In order to determine the magnitude of such payments, Table 5.4 provides some estimates of the government's strategy for dealing with over-employment in public enterprises. Assuming that the government continues with its divestment effort and privatizes all public enterprises, that public employees have on average 7.5 years of work experience, that the government follows its current practice of providing 5 months of wages for each year of service, and that 50 percent of the employees choose to take advantage of the retrenchment benefits, the government would have additional expenditures of more than 2.3 percent of GDP. Even if only 40 percent were to take advantage of the severance package, outlays would still amount to almost 2 percent of GDP. Although the Pakistani government would make only 50 percent of the payments while the buyers would cover the other 50 percent, the net wealth position of the government would deteriorate by the full amount, given that the buyers would reduce their bids to offset the additional cost. If the deterioration in the net wealth position of the government leads, for example, to higher taxes in the future, the generous retrenchment payments would tend to distort the economy.

To what degree the government would have to raise the financing directly or could rely on sales proceeds depends on the expected total sales price for the public entities still to be privatized. Data for the first wave of privatization show that the retrenchment costs amounted to 15 percent of the sales proceeds, of which 50 percent was directly financed by the government while the other 50 percent was covered by the investors.[124] In the absence of reliable data on the potential market value of the companies, data from profit and loss statements provide some, albeit limited, information. Based on such data for the enterprises still in the hands of the government and assuming that the net present value of the future stream of profits/losses is a multiple of this, the value of the assets would amount to about 0.4 percent of GDP. In effect, receipts from privatization would not cover the additional outlay and the government would have to raise the funds, perhaps through issuing more debt. Irrespective of whether the government finances the outlays by raising

---

[123] See Kemal (1994).

[124] See Privatisation Commission (1994).

Table 5.4. Pakistan: Retrenchment Costs

	Retrenchment in percent		
	30	40	50
	(In millions of rupees)		
For 5 years of service			
5 months wages	20,112	26,815	33,519
4 months wages	16,089	21,452	26,815
3 months wages	12,067	16,089	20,112
For 7.5 years of service			
5 months wages	30,167	40,223	50,279
4 months wages	24,134	32,178	40,223
3 months wages	18,100	24,134	30,167
For 10 years of service			
5 months wages	40,223	53,631	67,038
4 months wages	32,178	42,905	53,631
3 months wages	24,134	32,178	40,223
	(In percent of GDP)		
For 5 years of service			
5 months wages	0.9	1.2	1.5
4 months wages	0.7	1.0	1.2
3 months wages	0.6	0.7	0.9
For 7.5 years of service			
5 months wages	1.4	1.9	2.3
4 months wages	1.1	1.5	1.9
3 months wages	0.8	1.1	1.4
For 10 years of service			
5 months wages	1.9	2.5	3.1
4 months wages	1.5	2.0	2.5
3 months wages	1.1	1.5	1.9
Memorandum items:			
Public enterprise employment 1/	532,695	532,695	532,695
Employment reduction	159,809	213,078	266,348
Monthly average wage in rupees 2/	5,034	5,034	5,034
Nominal GDP	2,171,256	2,171,256	2,171,256

Source: Government of Pakistan. Public Sector Industries Annual Report; Government of Pakistan.
Government Sponsored Corporations; IMF. World Economic Outlook.

1/ Excluding employees that accepted retrenchment benefits in the first round of privatization.
2/ Since the reported average wage bill is inclusive of allowances and other benefits but the
retrenchment benefits are based on the basic salary, the average wage is reduced by
50 percent.

taxes or via the use of sales receipts, the magnitude of the retrenchment package is likely to have macroeconomic implications.

The extremely large retrenchment benefits in Pakistan transfer income and wealth to public sector employees at the expense of the average Pakistani citizen. Given the potential size of the transfers, the benefits add an additional burden to the fiscal position of the government and hence run counter to the goal of improving this fiscal position. Whether in the end the cost outweighs the benefit will depend on how efficiently the freed resources are used. In any case, the Pakistani approach to dealing with surplus workers represents a cost to society, and the question can be raised whether this cost can be justified as compensation for acquired rights, as discussed in the previous section. However, workers in public enterprises do not enjoy lifetime employment guarantees in Pakistan. In addition, the divestment of public enterprises and the acceptance of retrenchment benefits does not affect workers' rights to a retirement pension. Indeed, the magnitude of the "golden handshake" implies that a 55 year old worker who worked for 35 years for a public enterprise is not only entitled to a full pension at retirement age but also to a lump-sum payment of about 15 years of wages at the time of divestment. With respect to unemployment compensation, although Pakistan does not have a general unemployment insurance scheme—warranting some form of support to alleviate economic hardship—labor laws in Pakistan explicitly require companies to pay one month of severance payment for each year of service.[125] In summary, the magnitude of the retrenchment benefits cannot be justified on the basis of acquired rights or as a means of softening adverse social impacts of unemployment and hence largely represents an effort to buy out particular political groups.

5.4.4   The lack of transparency

The willingness of the government to offer generous transfer payments for political reasons was aided by the fact that at least initially, the sale of assets allowed the financing of the benefit packages without additional recourse to debt financing, which would have required budgetary approval. Furthermore, the Pakistani institutional set-up makes it costly for the public to scrutinize the fiscal implications of the buyout packages.

The lack of transparency occurs, on the one hand, as a result of the payment form. The agreement with the unions stipulates that 50 percent of the retrenchment costs must be borne by the investor. As a result, the investor's bidding price reflects a discount that is equivalent to the expected costs of making such retrenchment payments. In the absence of any market valuation of the public enterprises (for example, because of an earlier partial privatization and the consequent quotation on the stock exchange), the public remains uninformed about the implied fiscal implications of the buy-out. On the other hand, the lack of transparency also applies to the 50 percent of the outlays that are directly paid for by the government. As in

---

[125] It could, however, be debated whether the amount would be sufficient to provide social protection for workers with only a few years of work experience, who might require some additional support.

many countries, the government set up an extrabudgetary fund—the Privatization Commission—through which all privatization receipts are channeled. Consequently, the government can effectively make payments without having to go through a budget appropriations process. Privatization-related retrenchment benefits therefore do not undergo the same scrutiny as other government expenditures. A key mechanism for minimizing the cost of any politically motivated buyout is thereby rendered ineffective.

5.5   Summary

Privatization affects prices and inflation in a number of ways. With an unchanged monetary policy, privatization leads to a fall in prices if improvements in economic efficiency are associated with higher economic growth. Such an effect would, of course, take place over time. The sale of assets is, however, also likely to have an immediate impact on monetary aggregates. Governments that try to fight inflation could, for example, use the sale of assets to replace bank financing with financing from the sale of assets. While this would help policymakers temporarily lower inflation, it would not require the same fiscal adjustment that would be necessary without the privatization receipts.

Countries, especially those with pegged exchange rates, might be confronted by increases in base money and hence the money supply if privatization cause capital inflows. In order to maintain the peg, the central bank would have to engage in sterilized interventions. The potentially large capital inflows require that privatization is adequately taken into account in monetary management. At the same time, countries that are confronted with a reversal of capital flight either as a result of external factors or because of improvements in macroeconomic stabilization could be inclined to use the sale of assets as a means of mopping up liquidity. Countries with an underdeveloped market for government bonds or a large stock of debt might find the use of privatization as a substitute for open market operations particularly attractive. The same rationale applies if governments use privatization to alleviate the adverse monetary effects of debt-equity swaps.

The recent balance-of-payments and currency crises in emerging markets have resulted in another major wave of privatization. Even governments in East Asia that had been reluctant to allow foreign investors to own domestic companies and financial institutions have resorted to the sale of entities to foreign investors to attract "non-debt-creating capital inflows". While such sales might indeed lead to an improvement in the allocation of resources, given the economic crisis at hand, policymakers might instead engage in privatization strategies that are contrary to improving the growth potential of the economy.

Most of the evidence suggests that public enterprises suffer from over-employment and that large productivity gains can be made if private investors are able to bring real wages in line with marginal productivity. Although there may be some downward flexibility in real wages, given the magnitude of over-employment in some industries and companies, privatization is likely to have adverse employment effects. If privatization takes place in an environment of inefficient labor markets, unemployment might increase not only temporarily but also in the long term. Large-scale privatization should therefore go hand-in-hand with the labor market reforms.

Governments that are concerned with the political consequences of rising unemployment have incentives to minimize such short-term effects by engaging in activities that might undermine the very rationale for privatization. The evidence suggests that in a number of cases, governments have pursued employment guarantees from future investors, effectively delaying the restructuring process and hence the allocation of resources toward their most productive use. Furthermore, a number of governments have provided retrenchment packages and severance payments that exceed any amounts justified either on grounds of alleviating the adverse economic hardship as a result of layoffs or the buyout of previously acquired rights such as pension rights, lifetime employment guarantees, or implicit unemployment insurance.

As the case study on Pakistan suggests, the potential fiscal implications of extremely generous retrenchment programs can be large. Furthermore, the case study reveals that certain institutional set-ups are more likely to lead to such payments, given that these payments are not rigorously scrutinized by the public due to high information costs.

The example of Pakistan demonstrates how political considerations can cause governments to engage in activities that increase the liabilities of the government as a result of privatization. In this particular case, the government agreed to extremely generous retrenchment benefits to overcome political opposition to divestment because of adverse employment considerations. While the provision of retrenchment benefits is justifiable on the grounds of acquired rights and alleviation of economic hardship, the size of the benefits in Pakistan clearly undermines the benefits associated with privatization. Besides reallocating income and wealth toward employees or former employees of public enterprises at the expense of the general public, such large transfer payments can also have adverse macroeconomic implications. The lack of transparency and the institutional set-up in Pakistan also explain why governments face little public scrutiny and hence little political opposition when engaging in the buy-out of particular interest groups.

6 Modeling the Effects of Privatization

Given that the study intends to show why governments might rely on privatization in order to accomplish short-term macroeconomic objectives, the following section applies a framework that is frequently used by governments to evaluate short- and medium-term policy options. Despite its limitations[126], it can be used to illustrate quantitatively why policymakers might be inclined to use privatization to manage particular macroeconomic challenges and why they might be inclined to exploit privatization for short-term policy objectives. While the previous sections analyzed key macroeconomic aspects of privatization separately, the framework assures that fiscal, monetary, and balance-of-payments aspects of privatization are evaluated simultaneously.[127] In particular, the following model combines the accounting

---

[126] Mankiw (1990), for example, points out that despite substantial developments in economic theory and macroeconometric modeling since the 1970s, policymakers continue to rely on traditional frameworks such as the IS/LM model supplemented by the augmented Phillips curve. He argues that "the observation that recent developments have had little impact on applied macroeconomics creates at least the presumption that these developments are of little use to applied macroeconomists" (Mankiw, 1990: 1646) and uses a parable to clarify his point: "Nicholas Copernicus suggested that the sun, rather than the earth, is the center of the planetary system. ... Compared to the then prevailing geocentric system of Ptolemy, the original Copernican system was more elegant and, ultimately, it proved more useful. But at the time it was proposed and for many years thereafter, the Copernican system did not work as well as the Ptolemaic system. For predicting the positions of the planets, the Ptolemaic system was superior".

[127] Traditionally, the macroeconomy has been modeled in the form of a system of simultaneous equations in the tradition of Klein (1960) and the work at the Cowles Commission. However, the poor performance of large-scale simultaneous equations models during the stagflation of the 1970s and the developments in economic theory and econometrics since then have undermined the relevance and use of such models for both forecasting and policy analysis. As a result of these shortcomings, two other categories of macroeconometric models have become increasingly important over the past two decades: dynamic stochastic general equilibrium (DSGE) models and models based on vector autoregression techniques (VAR). Although DSGE models tend to be more satisfactory in terms of the clear identification of the long-run and short-run dynamics, the focus on real shocks and the emphasis on perfect markets have rendered them less effective in capturing short-term fluctuations caused by monetary shocks. While VARs have gained in importance

framework of a financial program[128] with the behavioral equations of a small-open economy.[129]

6.1   Outline of the framework

The framework is based on four accounting identities for the different sectors of the economy and equates the sources and uses of financial flows (see appendix). A deficit in one sector must be matched by a corresponding surplus in any of the others. In the case of the government sector, a budget deficit, defined as the difference between expenditures and tax revenues, must be financed externally by borrowing from the non-bank public through the issue of government securities or by obtaining credit from the banking system. (While in most industrialized countries the access of the government to central bank financing is limited, many developing countries have relied on the central bank for government financing.) The public sector identity also contains a variable that reflects the receipts from privatization given that governments have—as a result of the change in paradigm— an additional temporary source of financing.

The balance of payments identity expresses the external sector in terms of changes in net foreign assets. An external imbalance, reflecting a mismatch between exports and imports of goods and services as well as net transfers from abroad, is financed through capital inflows to the private sector or external borrowing by the public sector. In line with the accounts of the public sector, the balance of payments identity includes a privatization variable that reflects the sale of assets to foreigners.

---

for forecasting purposes, the lack of an economic structure, the data requirements, and the difficulty in interpreting impulse response functions in an economically meaningful manner have prevented them from becoming relevant for the analysis of policy options.

[128] Financial programs are based on an accounting framework that integrates the accounts of the key sectors of the economy: the real sector, the monetary accounts, the balance of payments, and the fiscal accounts. The framework ensures consistency across sectors. Financial programs usually rely on a set of behavioral equations that are either estimated empirically or imposed on the framework depending on data availability. In addition, these models incorporate detailed information on expected developments in particular sectors of the economy that enter the framework exogenously such as the expected availability of external official financing and one-time imports of large capital goods. The output of financial programming exercises is usually presented in a format that can be interpreted easily by policymakers, such as standard fiscal, monetary, and balance of payments tables. Financial programs are also the foundation for macroeconomic stabilization in the context of IMF programs. See Mikkelsen (1998); IMF (1996.2); and Wong and Pettersen (1979) on the concepts of financial programs.

[129] The model is similar that of Mundell-Fleming. However, while prices are sticky in the short-term, the model allows for price adjustments over time, permitting both output and prices to be determined endogenously. While economies such as the US, Germany, or Japan are more adequately represented by a model of a large open economy, some of the insights are applicable as well, albeit to a lesser degree.

The monetary sector is captured through the balance sheet of the financial system. In order to trace the causes of a monetary expansion, the assets side is analytically divided into net foreign assets, net credit to the private sector, and credit to the public sector. The last identity captures the real sector via the national income accounts.

The behavioral equations for the respective sectors of the economy are quite standard. The demand for real money balances depends on real income and the inflation rate. Inflation depends on both the supply of money and import prices expressed in domestic currency. Exports respond to changes in relative prices and the lag structure reflects the fact that exports adjust only partially within a given year. To reflect more adequately the fact that exports of natural resources priced in U.S. dollars are less responsive to changes in relative prices, the framework includes two export equations. The demand for imports is written as a function of both relative prices and the scale variable real domestic income. As a counterpart to the second export equation, the model includes an import equation for goods that are related to the production of exports of natural resources. Both import equations include a lag. Real investment is written as a function of real income.

The model also includes an equation for capacity output to reflect the supply side of the economy. Growth in capacity output depends on private investment and capital expenditure by the public sector, as well as labor force growth (reflected in the constant). Both private and government investment are assumed to impact potential output with a lag. Actual output is written as a function of capacity output and export demand. The impact of fiscal and monetary policy on output is captured through the inclusion of variables for excess money supply and government spending. Credit to the private sector and tax revenues depend on nominal income. In order to simulate a baseline scenario, it is assumed that the government maintains a roughly constant non-interest spending level in terms of GDP. The respective elasticities imposed on the system are in line with the parameters in similar models (Khan and Knight, 1991) and are given in Table 6.1.

Although the framework is designed to be representative and to demonstrate quantitatively and in a consistent manner the potential impacts of privatization, the behavioral equations reflect most closely those of developing countries and economies in transition. Some of the insights are applicable to industrialized countries as well, although to a lesser degree. In particular, Chapter 4 covers the political motives for large-scale privatization in industrialized countries that are not faced with the kind of economic constraints frequently found in developing and transition economies.

To allow for a detailed discussion of the various privatization scenarios and the respective motives for large-scale privatization, the base year data are drawn from Jamaica, a small open economy that faces a number of economic challenges,

Table 6.1. Model Parameters

Equation	Partial elasticities
Real exports 1 (non-bauxite)	
Relative export prices (current)	0.10
Relative export prices (lagged)	0.20
Relative export prices (lagged twice)	0.20
Real exports 2 (bauxite)	
Relative export prices (lagged twice)	0.10
Constant	2.50
Real imports 1 (non-bauxite)	
Real income	0.50
Relative import prices (current)	-0.20
Relative import prices (lagged)	-0.20
Real imports 2 (bauxite)	
Relative import prices (current)	-0.10
Constant	2.50
Capacity output	
Private investment (lagged)	0.10
Government capital expenditure (lagged)	0.10
Constant	1.00
Actual output	
Real exports	0.40
Real government expenditure	0.10
Excess money supply	0.10
Capacity output	0.50
Real private investment	
Real income	1.00
Inflation	
Money supply	0.80
Import prices	0.40
Real money demand	
Real output	1.10
Inflation	-0.20
Credit to the private sector	
Nominal GDP	1.00
Tax revenue 1 (non-import)	
Nominal GDP	0.95
Taxe revenue 2 (import)	
Imports	1.00
Government current expenditure	
Nominal GDP (lagged)	1.10
Government capital expenditure	
Nominal GDP (lagged)	1.10

including potential fiscal and balance-of-payments crises.[130] To demonstrate the use of privatization in the context of a balance-of-payments crisis, the model assumes a nominal exchange rate peg over the projection horizon. This analysis is also relevant to countries that rely on a more flexible exchange rate but that tend to intervene and could potentially resort to the sale of assets in order to stabilize the exchange rate.[131]

Two years prior to the base year (t), the government had embarked on a drastic but unbalanced anti-inflationary effort. While the central bank reduced the growth of base money substantially, the fiscal position moved from a surplus to a large deficit. Although the government was able to reduce inflation from 30 percent at the beginning of the anti-inflationary effort to slightly under 10 percent in t, the continued positive inflation differential between domestic prices and those of the country's trading partners in the context of a de-facto fixed exchange rate system led to an appreciation of the real exchange rate. The combined impact of the tight monetary and lax fiscal policy caused real interest rates to jump. This, combined with the loss in external competitiveness, led to a falloff in economic activity. Economic conditions worsened even further since the high real interest rates and the recession caused a financial sector crisis, prompting the government to provide financial support of around 30 percent of GDP to almost the entire domestic banking system as well as the largest insurance companies. As Tables A1-6 show, the country is faced with a base year fiscal deficit of almost 9 percent of GDP, a public debt stock of almost 120 percent, and a current account deficit reaching about 5.5 percent. Real economic output fell by 2.4 percent in t.[132]

6.2   Baseline scenario

To project the baseline scenario it is assumed that the government's economic policies remain largely unchanged, even if this implies a path of economic development that is unlikely to be sustainable. The baseline scenario will then serve as a benchmark to simulate the impact of the respective privatization scenarios. In particular, it is assumed that the central bank will continue with its relatively tight monetary policy in an attempt to reduce inflation to that of its trading partners by the later years of the projection horizon. Although the government is faced with large external amortization payments, it is assumed that the country will be able to roll over all external debt payments coming due. Furthermore, the baseline scenario assumes that the government will broadly maintain its import coverage of net international reserves. With respect to the fiscal accounts, it is assumed that the

---

[130] The choice of Jamaica for this purpose is also in line with the detailed country study in chapter 7. The data for the base year refer to fiscal year 1997/98 (fiscal years begin April 1) as provided by the Jamaican government and published by the IMF in the statistical appendix of the 1998 Selected Issues Paper (IMF 1998).

[131] The model is solved with the program M2. See Bier (1992).

[132] For a more detailed description of economic developments prior to the base year, see Economist Intelligence Unit (1998).

government will maintain current levels of both non-interest current expenditure and capital expenditure (in percent of GDP) over the projection period.[133]

As Figure 6.1 demonstrates, the country is confronted with an unsustainable policy path. Economic activity would remain depressed. While the government would be able to reduce inflation to that of its trading partners after five years—given the tight monetary policy and the positive impact of the fixed exchange rate on domestic prices—the real exchange rate would nevertheless appreciate for some time due to the still-positive inflation differential. As a result, export demand would remain sluggish. In addition, the continued anti-inflationary effort further dampens aggregate demand. As a result of the deterioration in competitiveness, the country is likely to be faced with a balance-of-payments crisis as shown by rising current account deficits and growing external financing gaps. As the public sector table A2 shows, the country is faced with a twin deficit. Besides the large and widening current account deficits, the already large fiscal deficits would increase further, as would the stock of total public debt, which would reach 133 percent of GDP in t+5. The associated high demands on real resources by the public sector would prevent real interest rates from subsiding and hence prevent a resumption of private sector activity. The baseline scenario suggests that in the absence of a policy change, the government would potentially have to monetize the deficit or default outright on its debt obligations.

In addition to the immediate financing problems the government faces, the rising current account deficit and the increased debt-to-GDP ratio could signal to investors the unsustainability of the government's current policy course and lead to a dramatic change in market sentiment at any time. Such a change in market sentiment would, of course, force the government to abandon its exchange rate peg and cause a disorderly adjustment process resulting in extreme economic hardship.

The illustrative baseline scenario thus calls for a major up-front change in economic policies to minimize the cost of adjustment in terms of economic welfare. However, the necessary measures would be politically extremely costly since they would include, for example, a dramatic reduction in non-interest government expenditure, a sharp increase in taxes, an up-front devaluation accompanied by fiscal measures, or any combination of the above. The incentive for politicians to search for politically less costly options are likely to be higher the closer the government is to facing re-election.

Faced with the kind of financing constraints mentioned above and a political environment that allows governments to sell public assets, governments have an incentive to privatize. While the sale of public enterprises might improve the structure of the economy, the allocation of resources, and hence medium-term growth potential, it is these short-term financing aspects that appear to make privatization especially attractive to policymakers. The following will demonstrate

---

[133] Given that the large support to the financial sector during the base year will lead to a dramatic jump in domestic interest payments in t+1, it is assumed that the government will accommodate this increase by cutting other current expenditure to avoid an even further increase in total public spending. The failure to do so would, of course, imply even larger fiscal deficits as well as larger financing gaps.

Figure 6.1. Simulation: Baseline Projection

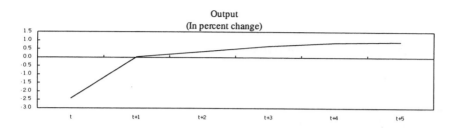

Output
(In percent change)

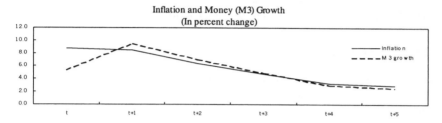

Inflation and Money (M3) Growth
(In percent change)

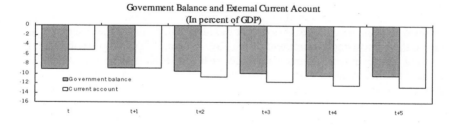

Government Balance and External Current Acount
(In percent of GDP)

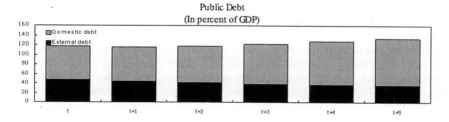

Public Debt
(In percent of GDP)

Sources: Table A1- A6.

the impact of three privatization scenarios and compare the outcome to the baseline scenario.

6.3   Privatization scenarios

Assuming that the focus of policymakers is on the short-term implications of privatization, the following scenarios establish the impact of a reduction in government debt as a result of the sale of public assets. The model is used to determine quantitatively the implications of fiscal expansion as well as monetary contraction. The size of the privatization receipts is based on experiences with large-scale privatizations in number of countries as discussed in chapter 4.

6.3.1   Asset swaps

In order to maximize the net wealth position of the government, the receipts from the sale of public assets should be used to retire government debt. Private investors would merely exchange their holdings of government debt for equity. In a world of perfect capital markets in which the risk-adjusted return on assets is identical, such an asset swap would leave the net wealth position of the government unchanged. A reduction in assets is matched by a similar reduction in liabilities. In the same vein, to show that the sale of assets does not fundamentally change the fiscal stance and hence the borrowing requirement of the government, it is usually argued that, from a fiscal standpoint, governments should treat the receipts from privatization as a form of financing rather than as a revenue item.[134] Unlike taxes, which are a form of genuine income for the government, the sale of government assets is conceptually speaking similar to borrowing, although in the case of divestment, the government borrows against the future stream of income from its assets. This, of course, assumes that the sales price of the asset is positive.

The assumption of perfect capital markets is, of course, extreme, especially as it relates to developing countries and transition economies. Furthermore, the internal rate of return on government investments is often substantially less than the government's borrowing cost. Hence, the falloff in dividends and transfers from, for example, public entities to the government can be assumed to be substantially less than the interest cost that government budgets carry on their outstanding debt stock. Cash-strapped governments could opt to divest their assets, reduce their debt stocks and therefore reduce the current fiscal deficit and financing requirements. In case of the illustrative economy which in t carries a debt stock of about 117 percent of GDP, a reduction of the domestic debt stock equal to 3.5 percent of GDP would imply—with a real interest rate assumption of some 12 percent—an improvement in the budget deficit of less than 0.5 percent of GDP.

---

[134] See Vickers and Yarrow (1998).

Since such an asset swap would result in an improvement of the fiscal position in t+1 only at the margin—compared to the overall size of the fiscal deficit—governments have incentives to use the full amount of the sales proceeds to finance the budget directly. Doing so would, of course, imply that the net-wealth position of the government deteriorates. Countries that are faced with real financing gaps and borrowing constraints—both abroad and domestically—are especially likely to use privatization receipts to finance the operations of the public sector. As the fiscal section showed, the magnitude of some of the privatization programs reduces the one-period budget constraints of many countries considerably.

6.3.2   Privatization and fiscal expansion

As indicated in the chapter on the politics of macroeconomic policymaking, privatization gives governments an additional instrument to influence aggregate variables at little political cost. In particular, the availability of additional resources could encourage policymakers to increase government spending above and beyond what would otherwise be possible.

To simulate the impact of such a policy on a small open economy, it is assumed that the government will divest assets valued at 3.5 percent of GDP during period t+1, allowing it to increase government spending accordingly. Since most governments are likely to avoid raising the publicly visible fiscal deficit, the exercise assumes that the receipts from privatization are treated as an above-the-line item, leaving the public borrowing requirement unchanged.[135]

As Figure 6.2 and summary Table A7 show, the privatization-financed increase in government spending leads to the expected improvement in aggregate demand, causing output in t+1 to increase by about 1 percentage point compared to the baseline scenario. As a result of the increase in domestic demand, imports increase and the current account deteriorates slightly. The improvement in actual output causes the fiscal deficit as a percent of GDP to fall marginally, due to the fact that both capital expenditures and interest payments in t+1 are largely fixed in nominal terms.

This scenario is based on the assumption that the government uses privatization receipts to increase government spending only once and from t+2 onward reverts to its pre-privatization spending level. The resulting fiscal contraction is, of course, associated with an adverse impact on output. Alternatively, this scenario demonstrates how fiscally constrained governments could use "windfall profits" from privatization to boost economic activity prior to elections, along the lines of the political business cycle literature. That is, the primary motive for privatization might be associated with fiscal management—to increase output and reduce unemployment temporarily—rather than with efficiency or structural adjustment

---

[135] Some countries, however, are institutionally constrained from treating privatization receipts as revenue equivalent in their budget. As will be discussed in the fiscal section, countries that wanted to meet the Maastricht deficit criteria for entering EMU were eventually prevented from using privatization receipts as a revenue item.

Figure 6.2. Privatization and Fiscal Expansion in t+1
(Difference to baseline scenario)

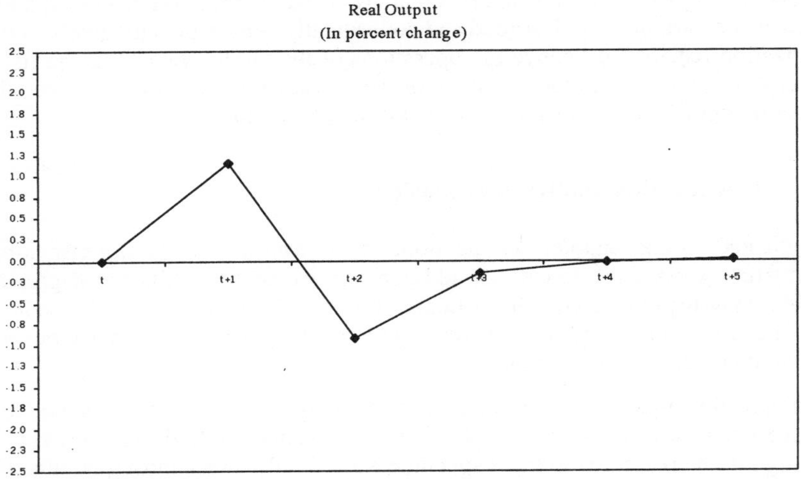

Real Output
(In percent change)

Sources: Table A 7.

considerations. Furthermore—as will be discussed more thoroughly in the fiscal section—the high percentage of public assets in many countries would allow their governments to sustain higher spending levels for some time, further postponing the resulting fiscal contraction.

6.3.3   Privatization and the fight against inflation

Many developing countries and transition economies experienced periods of high inflation. Most often, these inflationary periods are associated with fiscal imbalances that cause governments to resort to the printing press. The fight against inflation is hence most often associated with fiscal consolidation. While reducing inflation may be popular, especially in the aftermath of hyperinflations, the required fiscal adjustment is certainly not. The temporary availability of public assets allows policymakers to substitute the monetization of government deficits through the sale of assets. Doing so allows governments—at least temporarily—to reduce inflation without having to address the underlying fiscal imbalances. Again, privatization might be driven primarily by short-term political considerations.

The following scenario shows the attractiveness of public assets in the short-term fight against inflation in the context of the illustrative framework. As compared to the baseline scenario, the government sells assets equivalent to 3.5 percent of GDP in t+1. The government uses the resources to finance part of the public deficit instead of relying on financing from the banking system. With a given change in net foreign assets and broadly unchanged credit to the private sector, the reduction in net credit to the government implies a slowdown in the growth of money. As a result, the government is temporarily able to improve its inflation performance in t+1 (see Figure 6.3) without having to improve its overall fiscal position. Although the monetary contraction tends to have an adverse impact on economic activity via the excess money supply variable, the more rapid reduction in inflation avoids a further appreciation of the real exchange rate and improves the country's external competitiveness. The improved export performance is reflected in a smaller current account deficit and outweighs the adverse monetary impact, leading to an overall increase in economic activity. While real economic activity is higher than in the baseline scenario, the lower inflation rate is associated with lower nominal GDP. Since non-interest government expenditure is assumed to be the same in both scenarios, the fiscal deficit measured as a percentage of GDP is higher.

As in the expansionary fiscal scenario, it is assumed that the government sells assets only in t+1 and then reverts back to its original path of bank financing causing inflation to pick up again in succeeding years. Of course, additional sales of assets in future years would allow the government to maintain the lower inflation rate for a longer period of time without having to tackle the underlying fiscal imbalances.

6.4   Summary

It has been argued that governments that are confronted with an unsustainable policy path might have an incentive to opt for privatization in order to postpone politically unpopular adjustment measures. In such circumstances, privatization might prevent or delay economic reforms rather than be a key instrument of reform. In order to illustrate these incentives, a framework was applied that is frequently used by governments to design adjustment programs and to evaluate policy options. While such financial programs often rely on exogenous assumptions about inflation and growth, the framework includes a number of simple behavioral equations that allow for the endogenous determination of both variables. Despite the limited predictive power of the framework, it helps to quantify in a consistent manner key variables that policymakers use for their decision-making.

Using such a framework and inputting data from a small open economy that faces a number of economic challenges, a baseline scenario was developed that projects the main macroeconomic accounts and variables on the assumption of unchanged government policies. The projections reveal that the economy is faced with growing external and fiscal financing gaps as well as an increase in the public debt stock. All of the above seem to suggest that the country is on an unsustainable policy course. While immediate action would minimize the welfare loss, the scenario demonstrated that the government could engage in an aggressive privatization program to address both the external and domestic financing gaps. By doing so it might be inclined to divest of its assets and entities in such a way that minimizes the financing gaps but that prevents the economy from restructuring.

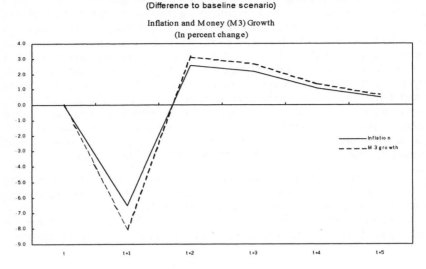

Figure 6.3. Privatization and Monetary Contraction in t+1
(Difference to baseline scenario)

Inflation and Money (M3) Growth
(In percent change)

Sources: Table A 8.

In addition to the merely cash-flow considerations of privatization, governments might embrace privatization to affect economic output and inflation in the short term. The rationale for such an endeavor is that a lower inflation rate or higher economic growth and hence less unemployment might correlate positively with the probability of getting re-elected. Based on the assumption that the government sells assets worth 3.5 percent of GDP, the fiscal expansion scenario showed that economic output could temporarily be increased by about 1 percent in t+1. The second scenario was also based on the assumption that the government can sell assets on the order of 3.5 percent of GDP. This time the resources were used to substitute for the financing of the public deficit via the banking system. The illustrative example showed that policymakers that might profit politically from reducing inflation could do so without having to undertake the necessary but politically costly fiscal reforms.

6.5 Appendix

Table A1. Simulation: Balance of Payments
Baseline projections

	t	t+1	t+2	t+3	t+4	t+5
(In millions of U.S. dollars)						
Current account	**-361**	**-646**	**-815**	**-949**	**-1046**	**-1117**
Exports of goods	1398	1431	1455	1491	1537	1592
Non-bauxite exports	655	657	653	655	664	677
Bauxite exports	743	774	803	836	873	915
Imports of goods	3104	3270	3421	3560	3686	3805
Non-bauxite imports	2918	3074	3214	3342	3457	3564
Bauxite imports	186	196	207	218	229	241
Nonfactor services credit	1686	1725	1753	1795	1849	1913
Nonfactor services debit	863	908	949	986	1020	1052
Interest payments private (net)	-47	97	125	158	194	232
Interest payments public (net)	155	174	192	209	227	245
Transfers (net)	630	646	662	678	695	713
Capital account	**308**	**211**	**265**	**294**	**294**	**353**
Capital account	308	211	265	294	294	353
Official capital	80	1	1	1	1	1
Disbursements	342	262	262	262	262	262
Privatization receipts, foreign	*0*	*0*	*0*	*0*	*0*	*0*
Amortization	261	261	261	261	261	261
Private capital inflow (net) 1/	228	210	264	293	293	352
Overall balance	**-53**	**40**	**40**	**40**	**40**	**40**
Financing gap	**0**	**475**	**591**	**695**	**792**	**804**
Memorandum items: ·						
Current account in percent of GDP	-5.4	-9.0	-10.6	-11.7	-12.4	-12.8
Change in NIR	-53	40	40	40	40	40
NIR in millions of U.S. dollar	541	581	621	661	701	741
NIR in months of non-bauxite imports (goods and NFS)	1.2	1.2	1.2	1.3	1.3	1.3
Public foreign debt (in millions U.S. dollar)	3173	3173	3173	3173	3173	3173
Debt service ratio (in percent of goods and NFS)	13.5	13.9	14.4	14.8	15.1	15.2
Exchange rate (local currency per U.S. dollar)	36.5	36.5	36.5	36.5	36.5	36.5
Domestic price index	100.0	108.5	115.4	120.8	124.7	128.3
World price index	100.0	102.5	105.0	107.6	110.2	112.9
Real exchange rate index	100.0	105.8	109.8	112.2	113.0	113.5
Export price index	100.0	102.4	100.9	99.4	97.9	96.4
Import price index	100.0	97.5	95.1	92.7	90.4	88.1
Terms of trade	100.0	100.0	100.0	100.0	100.0	100

Source: IMF, 1998. Jamaica—Selected Issues. IMF Staff Country Reports 99/02 and projections.

1/ Including other public sector inflows

Table A 2. Simulation: Public Sector Accounts
Baseline projections

	t	t+1	t+2	t+3	t+4	t+5
	(In local currency)					
Total revenue	66081	70807	74891	78407	81243	83956
Tax on imports	17167	18059	18868	19615	20290	20923
Other taxes	48913	52747	56022	58791	60952	63032
Privatization receipts, total	*1*	*1*	*1*	*1*	*1*	*1*
Total expenditure	87516	94385	101607	107784	113016	117174
Current expenditure	72113	77627	83425	88445	92773	96278
Non-interest expenditure	47538	41911	44264	46755	48670	50210
Interest 1/	24575	35716	39161	41690	44103	46068
Capital expenditure 2/	15403	16758	18182	19338	20242	20895
Current balance	-6032	-6821	-8535	-10039	-11531	-12323
Primary balance	3140	16	15	12313	12330	12850
Operational balance	-10743	-21851	-26310	-17875	-22109	-23440
Overall balance	-21435	-23579	-26717	-29378	-31774	-33219
Financing	21435	23579	26717	29378	31774	33219
Foreign financing	2933	30	30	30	30	30
Domestic financing	18502	6196	5123	3978	2853	3840
Bank financing 3/	17653	2800	1727	582	-543	-744
Non-bank financing	849	3396	3396	3396	3396	4584
Financing gap	0	17351	21562	25368	28890	29347
	(In percent of GDP)					
Total revenue	27.2	26.9	26.7	26.5	26.4	26.3
Tax on imports	7.1	6.9	6.7	6.6	6.6	6.6
Other taxes	20.2	20.0	19.9	19.9	19.8	19.7
Privatization receipts, total	*0.0*	*0.0*	*0.0*	*0.0*	*0.0*	*0.0*
Total expenditure	36.1	35.9	36.2	36.4	36.7	36.7
Current expenditure	29.7	29.5	29.7	29.9	30.1	30.2
Non-interest expenditure	19.6	15.9	15.8	15.8	15.8	15.7
Interest 1/	10.1	13.6	13.9	14.1	14.3	14.4
Capital expenditure 2/	6.3	6.4	6.5	6.5	6.6	6.5
Current balance	-2.5	-2.6	-3.0	-3.4	-3.7	-3.9
Primary balance	1.3	0.0	0.0	4.2	4.0	4.0
Operational balance	-4.4	-8.3	-9.4	-6.0	-7.2	-7.3
Overall balance	-8.8	-9.0	-9.5	-9.9	-10.3	-10.4
Financing	8.8	9.0	9.5	9.9	10.3	10.4
Foreign financing	1.2	0.0	0.0	0.0	0.0	0.0
Domestic financing	7.6	2.4	1.8	1.3	0.9	1.2
Bank financing 3/	7.3	1.1	0.6	0.2	-0.2	-0.2
Non-bank financing	0.3	1.3	1.2	1.1	1.1	1.4
Financing gap	0.0	6.6	7.7	8.6	9.4	9.2

Sources: IMF, 1998. Jamaica--Selected Issues. IMF Staff Country Reports 99/02 and projections.

1/ The jump in domestic interest payments from t to $t+1$ is the result of the financial sector bailout. Interest payments on debt issued in t become due only in $t+1$.

2/ The statistical discrepancy between fiscal data and financing data from the banking system is allocated toward capital expenditure.

3/ While in the base year most of the government deficit was financed through a drawdown in government deposits at the central bank, an increase in liquidity was prevented through sterilization.

Table A 3. Simulation: Summary Accounts of the Banking System
Baseline projections

	t	t+1	t+2	t+3	t+4	t+5
(In local currency)						
Net foreign assets	23426	24886	26346	27806	29266	30726
Net domestic assets	81551	87943	92770	95999	97534	98786
Net credit to the public sector	39687	42487	44214	44796	44253	43509
Credit to the private sector	41864	45456	48556	51203	53281	55277
Money supply (M3)	82329	90181	96468	101157	104152	106864
Change in net foreign assets	-1922	1460	1460	1460	1460	1460
Change in net domestic assests	11660	6392	4827	3229	1535	1252
Change in net credit to the public sector	17653	2800	1727	582	-543	-744
Change in credit to the private sector	-5993	3592	3100	2647	2078	1996
Change in money supply (M3)	4130	7852	6287	4689	2995	2712
		15.5	15			
(In percent change) 1/						
Change in net foreign assets	-2.5	1.8	1.6	1.5	1.4	1.4
Change in net domestic assests	14.9	7.8	5.4	3.3	1.5	1.2
Change in credit to the public sector	22.6	3.4	1.9	0.6	-0.5	-0.7
Change in credit to the private sector	-7.7	4.4	3.4	2.7	2.1	1.9
Change in money supply (M3)	9.0	9.5	7.0	4.9	3.0	2.6
Memorandum item:						
Multiplier	2.67	2.67	2.67	2.67	2.67	2.67
Base Money	30835	33776	36130	37887	39008	40024
Real money supply	82329	90181	96468	101157	104152	106864
Real money demand	82329	82459	83136	84020	84974	85695

1/ In relation to the stock of money (M3) at the beginning of the period.

Sources: IMF. 1998. Jamaica—Selected Issues. IMF Staff Country Reports 99/02 and projections.

Table A 4. Simulation: National Accounts
Baseline projections

	t	t+1	t+2	t+3	t+4	t+5
(In local currency at current market prices)						
GDP	242612	263234	280956	296013	307793	319150
Private consumption	162906	179846	193882	205166	213117	220736
Private investment	30077	32633	34826	36686	38138	39537
Public current expenditure	66456	71281	76431	80804	84484	87341
Public investment	15403	16758	18182	19338	20242	20895
Exports	51026	52243	53123	54432	56106	58095
Imports	113296	119356	124863	129951	134552	138875
Non-factor services, net	30040	29829	29375	29537	30257	31420
Disposable income	201241	212470	225659	236587	244867	252733
(In percent of GDP)						
GDP	100	100	100	100	100	100
Private consumption	67.1	68.3	69.0	69.3	69.2	69.2
Private investment	12.4	12.4	12.4	12.4	12.4	12.4
Public current expenditure	27.4	27.1	27.2	27.3	27.4	27.4
Public investment	6.3	6.4	6.5	6.5	6.6	6.5
Exports	21.0	19.8	18.9	18.4	18.2	18.2
Imports	46.7	45.3	44.4	43.9	43.7	43.5
Non-factor services, net	12.4	11.3	10.5	10.0	9.8	9.8
Disposable income	82.9	80.7	80.3	79.9	79.6	79.2
(In local currency at constant prices, t = base year)						
Real GDP	242612	242721	243545	245218	247360	249593
Productive capacity	242612	243075	245582	248611	251661	254743
Private consumption	162906	165756	168008	169839	170903	172046
Private investment	30077	30090	30189	30390	30648	30918
Public current expenditure	66456	65696	66231	66890	67749	68075
Public investment	15403	15445	15755	16008	16232	16286
Imports	113296	116445	118846	120673	121898	122744
Exports	51026	50969	50563	50544	50828	51345
Memorandum items:						
Real GDP growth	-2.4	0.0	0.3	0.7	0.9	0.9
Inflation rate	8.8	8.5	6.4	4.7	3.2	2.9

Source: IMF. 1998. Jamaica--Selected Issues. IMF Staff Country Reports 99/02 and projections.

Table A 5. Simulation: Public Debt
Baseline projections

	t	t+1	t+2	t+3	t+4	t+5
(In Jamaica dollars)						
Total debt	284554	305301	330259	359023	391309	425240
External debt	115815	115815	115815	115815	115815	115815
Domestic debt	168739	189486	214444	243208	275494	309425
(In percent of GDP)						
Total debt	117.3	116.0	117.5	121.3	127.1	133.2
External debt	47.7	44.0	41.2	39.1	37.6	36.3
Domestic debt	69.6	72.0	76.3	82.2	89.5	97.0
Memorandum items:						
External debt (in US$)	3173	3173	3173	3173	3173	3173
Exchange rate (J$ per US$)	36.5	36.5	36.5	36.5	36.5	36.5
Real effective interest rate 1/	12.9	15.5	15.0	14.0	13.0	12.0
Nominal interest rate	22.8	25.3	22.3	19.3	16.6	15.2
Domestic interest payments	18918	29370	32167	34049	35814	37131
Nominal GDP	242612	263234	280956	296013	307793	319150

Source: IMF, 1998. Jamaica--Selected Issues. IMF Staff Country Reports 99/02 and projections.

1/ The interest rate substantially less in t since the issue of debt for the bailout of the financial sector in t starts to accure interest in t+1.

Table A 6. Simulation: Assumptions
Baseline projections

	t+1	t+2	t+3	t+4	t+5
Public sector external amortization (in million US$)	261	261	261	261	261
Public sector external borrowing (in milllion US$)	262	262	262	262	262
Public sector non-bank borrowing (in million J$)	3396	3396	3396	3396	4584
Change in net foreign assets (in million US$)	40	40	40	40	40
Capital expenditure (in percent of GDP)	6.4	6.5	6.5	6.6	6.5
Privatization receipts (in percent of GDP)	0	0	0	0	0
Exchange rate (local currency per US$)	36.5	36.5	36.5	36.5	36.5
World prices (percent change)	2.5	2.5	2.5	2.5	2.5
Import prices (percent change)	2.5	2.5	2.5	2.5	2.5
Export prices (percent change)	2.5	2.5	2.5	2.5	2.5
Foreign interest rate (old debt)	5.0	5.0	5.0	5.0	5.0
Foreign interest rate (new debt)	12.0	12.0	12.0	12.0	12.0
Foreign transfers (percent change)	0.2	15.5	15.0	2.0	1.5

Table A 7. Simulation: Summary Indicators
Privatization and Fiscal Expansion in t+1

	t	t+1	t+2	t+3	t+4	t+5
(Percentage change)						
Real sector						
GDP (real growth)	-2.4	1.2	-0.6	0.5	0.8	0.9
Consumer price inflation (end-of-period)	8.8	8.5	7.0	5.0	3.4	3.0
External sector						
Exchange rate (local currency per U.S. dollar)	36.5	36.5	36.5	36.5	36.5	36.5
Real effective exchange rate (1993-94=100)	151.2	160.2	167.1	171.2	172.6	173.3
External current account (in percent of GDP)	-5.4	-9.2	-10.6	-11.8	-12.6	-13.0
of which						
Exports	21.0	19.6	18.7	18.2	18.0	17.9
Imports	46.7	45.0	44.1	43.6	43.4	43.2
Nonfactor services (net)	15.5	15.0	9.5	9.2	9.2	9.5
Changes in net international reserves (in million U.S. dolla	-53	40	40	40	40	40
Privatization receipts, foreign (in percent of GDP)	0	0	0	0	0	0
Financing gap (in million U.S. dollar)	0	499	601	714	819	837
External debt service ratio						
(in percent of exports of goods and NFS)	13.5	13.9	14.4	14.8	15.1	15.3
(In percent of GDP)						
Public sector						
Central government revenue	27.2	30.3	26.6	26.4	26.3	26.2
Privatization receipts, total	*0.0*	*3.5*	*0.0*	*0.0*	*0.0*	*0.0*
Central government expenditure	36.1	39.3	36.5	36.6	36.9	36.9
of which						
Interest payments	10.1	16.3	15.8	15.2	15.1	15.1
Central government primary balance	1.3	0.0	0.0	5.1	4.5	4.5
Central government balance	-8.8	-9.0	-9.9	-10.2	-10.6	-10.7
Financing	8.8	9.0	9.9	10.2	10.6	10.7
External	1.2	0.0	0.0	0.0	0.0	0.0
Domestic	7.6	2.1	2.1	1.4	1.0	1.2
Statistical discrepancy	0.0	6.8	7.7	8.7	9.6	9.4
Bank financing	7.3	0.9	0.9	0.3	-0.1	-0.2
Non-bank financing	0.3	1.3	1.2	1.1	1.1	1.4
Privatization receipts, total	0.0	0.0	0.0	0.0	0.0	0.0
Financing gap	0.0	6.8	7.7	8.7	9.6	9.4
Public sector debt (in percent of GDP)	117.3	114.7	116.9	120.7	126.6	132.9
Memorandum items:						
Broad money growth (percentage change, end-of-period	9.0	9.6	7.7	5.2	3.1	2.7

Sources: Table A1- A6 and projections.

Table A 8. Simulation: Summary Indicators
Privatization and Monetary Contraction in t+1

	t	t+1	t+2	t+3	t+4	t+5
(Percentage change)						
Real sector						
GDP (real growth)	-2.4	0.6	0.2	0.5	0.7	0.8
Consumer price inflation (end-of-period)	8.8	2.0	8.9	6.8	4.3	3.4
External sector						
Exchange rate (local currency per U.S. dollar)	36.5	36.5	36.5	36.5	36.5	36.5
Real effective exchange rate (1993-94=100)	151.2	150.5	159.9	166.7	169.6	171.1
External current account (in percent of GDP)	-5.4	-8.8	-9.5	-10.7	-11.9	-12.5
of which						
Exports	21.0	21.1	19.8	19.0	18.5	18.4
Imports	46.7	47.5	45.2	44.2	43.9	43.6
Nonfactor services (net)	15.5	15.0	10.4	10.0	9.8	9.9
Changes in net international reserves (in US$ million)	-53	40	40	40	40	40
Privatization receipts, foreign (in percent of GDP)	0	0	0	0	0	0
Financing gap (in million US dollar)	0	426	483	600	740	779
External debt service ratio						
(in percent of exports of goods and NFS)	13.5	13.9	14.3	14.6	14.9	15.2
(In percent of GDP)						
Public sector						
Central government revenue	27.2	27.3	26.8	26.6	26.4	26.3
Privatization receipts, total	0.0	0.0	0.0	0.0	0.0	0.0
Central government expenditure	36.1	38.0	35.7	36.0	36.5	36.6
Non-interest current	19.6	18.7	10.9	12.3	13.9	14.6
of which						
Interest payments	10.1	12.6	18.5	17.3	16.1	15.5
Central government primary balance	1.3	0.0	0.0	7.9	6.0	5.2
Central government balance	-8.8	-10.6	-8.9	-9.4	-10.1	-10.3
External	1.2	0.0	0.0	0.0	0.0	0.0
Domestic	7.6	4.4	2.4	1.9	1.2	1.3
Bank financing	7.3	-0.5	1.1	0.7	0.1	-0.1
Non-bank financing	0.3	1.4	1.3	1.2	1.1	1.4
Privatization receipts, total	0.0	3.5	0.0	0.0	0.0	0.0
Financing gap	0.0	6.3	6.5	7.5	8.9	8.9
Public sector debt	117.3	122.1	122.9	123.2	127.5	132.8
Memorandum items:						
Broad money growth (percentage change, end-of-perio	9.0	1.5	10.1	7.5	4.3	3.2

Sources: Table A1- A6 and projections.

Balance sheet identities

National accounts

$$Y \equiv CP + IP + CG + IG + X_i - IM_i$$

Government sector

$$G \equiv T_i + BD + CAPF + NDCG + PR$$

Monetary sector

$$M \equiv NFA + NDCP + DCP$$

External sector

$$\Delta NFA \equiv X_i - IM_i - INTG - INTP + CAPF + CAPP + TR + PRF$$

Behavioral equations[136]

$$\Delta \log P_t = \alpha_1 \Delta \log IMP_t + \alpha_2 REMS_t$$

$$\Delta \log y_t = \alpha_3 \Delta \log x_t + \alpha_4 \Delta \log g_t + \alpha_5 \Delta \log y_t^* + \alpha_6 REMS_t$$

$$\Delta \log y_t^* = \alpha_7 \Delta \log ip_t + \alpha_8 \Delta \log ig_t$$

$$\Delta \log im_{it} = a \Delta \log RPIM_t + a \Delta \log y_t$$

$$\Delta \log x_{it} = \alpha_9 \Delta \log RPX_t$$

$$\Delta \log ip_t = \alpha_{10} \Delta \log y_t$$

$$\Delta \log T_{it} = \alpha_{11} \Delta \log Y_t$$

$$\Delta \log IG_t = \alpha_{12} \Delta \log Y_t$$

$$\Delta \log CG_t = \alpha_{13} \Delta \log Y_t$$

$$\Delta \log DCP_t = \alpha_{14} \Delta \log Y_t$$

---

[136] The solution technique of the program requires that all variables are specified in terms of percentage changes.

$$\Delta \log D_t = \alpha_{15} \Delta \log Y_t$$

Definitional equations

$$G \equiv CG + IG + INT$$

$$PR \equiv PRF + PFD$$

$$RPIM \equiv \frac{PIM * NER}{P}$$

$$RPX \equiv \frac{PX * NER}{P}$$

$$NER \equiv J\$ / US\$$$

$$RER \equiv \frac{P}{P^* * NER}$$

$$REMS \equiv \frac{M - MD_{t-1}}{MD_{t-1}}$$

Variable names

BD	Domestic non-bank borrowing
$CAPF$	Official capital inflow
$CAPP$	Private capital inflow
CG	Government consumption
CP	Private consumption
DCP	Domestic credit to the private sector (stock)
G	Total government spending
IG	Government capital expenditure
IM	Imports of goods and non-factor services
INT	Public foreign interest payments
$INTP$	Private foreign interest and divident payments
IP	Private investment

M	Money
md	Real money demand
Mm	Real money
$NDCG$	Net domestic credit to the government (stock)
NER	Nominal exchange rate
NFA	Net foreign assets (stock)
P	Domestic prices
P^*	Foreign prices
PR	Total privatization receipts
PRF	Privatization receipts from abroad
$REMS$	Excess money supply
RER	Real exchange rate
$RPIM$	Relative import prices
RPX	Relative export prices
T	Government revenue excluding privatization receipts
TR	Transfers
TR	Transfers
X	Exports of goods and non-factor services
Y	Nominal GDP
y	Real actual output
y^*	Real capacity output

7   Coming Full Circle: The Case of Jamaica

Because little time has passed since the start of the almost universal privatization wave, and many countries are still in the midst of their privatization efforts, the evidence of large-scale privatization failures is still scant. Moreover, the possibility of a reversal of the current privatization wave seems remote. While the following case study on Jamaica is certainly unique, it has been selected to demonstrate how the use of privatization as an instrument for short-term objectives can impede reforms necessary for improving the economy's growth prospects. As a result, the country has come full circle and re-nationalized many of the companies that had been transferred to the private sector only a couple of years ago. Despite the fact that Jamaica started to transfer ownership to the private sector ahead of many other countries in the region, policymakers of successive governments remained suspicious of the private sector. In many respects, Jamaica has been the largest privatization failure so far and provides some insights into the pitfalls of ill-conceived privatization strategies. It also demonstrates how indicators of the extent of privatization—such as the number of entities formally owned by the government or the number of publicly employed people—can be misleading. It is an especially telling case since the country embarked on its privatization effort early on and was once considered a model case by both the Reagan and the Thatcher administrations.

7.1   Background

During the first decade following Jamaica's independence in 1962, government activity in the economy was limited, focusing on the maintenance of stable fiscal and monetary policies, the establishment of regulatory agencies, and the enforcement of property rights.[137] However, economic growth was driven by investments in capital- rather than labor-intensive industries; certain sectors such as agriculture even experienced drops in output. Despite large growth rates, both

---

[137] See IMF (1998.2).

income inequality and unemployment were rising. Government efforts to rectify some of the social disparity increased in early 1972 after the more left-wing Peoples National Party (PNP) achieved power. During the 1970s the role of the public sector increased substantially as a result of an inward-looking and protectionist economic policy. After a wave of nationalizations, key sectors of the Jamaican economy such as textiles, sugar, bauxite, financial institutions and hotels ended up in the hands of the government. According to the 1984 registry of public entities, the government owned some 199 public enterprises.[138] At its peak, government expenditure amounted to almost 45 percent of GDP. While overall employment data for the public sector are not available, the central government alone employed some 12 percent of the labor force in 1979.[139] As figure 7.1 shows, from the mid-1980s onward, Jamaica embarked on a divestment program that spanned more than a decade. Between 1985 and 1997, successive governments divested some 66 public entities. Total receipts from the sale of government assets, including the divestment of property, amount to some 13 percent of GDP cumulatively.[140] The formal retrenchment of government activity in the production of goods and services is reflected in declines in both public sector employment and the contribution of government output to total value added, with the latter falling to less than 30 percent in the early 1990s. In addition to privatization, the government also liberalized the economy by eliminating price and foreign exchange controls. Formally, most indicators suggest that the Jamaican economy has undergone serious structural changes over the past decade and that government intervention has been reduced substantially. Nevertheless, economic performance has remained subdued. With the exception of a spurt in economic growth in the second half of the 1980s following a major devaluation, economic output has been sluggish (see table 7.1).[141] In effect, economic growth in the 1990s has been stagnant. Overall, the level of output in real terms in 1998 was almost unchanged from its level in 1973, implying a decline in output per capita of around 28 percent over the same period. Other indicators of economic well-being, such as the number of people per physician, have also deteriorated over the years. Given the formal rationalization of the economy, one would have expected an improvement in growth performance. Instead, Jamaica represents a growth puzzle.

7.2   The role of the government and Jamaica's growth puzzle

The causes of Jamaica's poor growth performance are many. One contributing factor is the country's frequent changes in fiscal, monetary, and exchange rate

---

[138] See Schumacher and Hutchinson (1991).

[139] See IMF (1998.2).

[140] This figure represents each year's privatization receipts as a percentage of that year's GDP, summed over the period from 1981 to 1997.

[141] The National Accounts Statistics in Jamaica are poor. GDP might be underestimated substantially and a large part of economic activity might be unrecorded.

Figure 7.1. Jamaica: Privatization, 1981-97

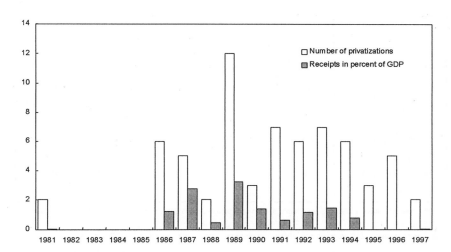

Sources: IMF, 1998.

policy. These policy shifts, along with high and varying degrees of inflation, have created uncertainty and prevented the economy from reaching its long-run growth potential. In the past, macroeconomic adjustment efforts were frequently abandoned prematurely, suggesting adjustment fatigue, only to be followed by another round of stabilization. This is, for example, reflected by the fact that over the course of some 25 years, Jamaica had nine standby arrangements and four programs under the extended fund facility from the IMF, as well as eleven structural adjustment loans from the World Bank. Jamaica's most recent anti-inflationary program has already caused output to fall for three consecutive years.[142] Besides Jamaica's tendency to engage in "stop-and-go" policy, it appears that many of the past decade's structural reforms were implemented half-heartedly. The question arises as to what degree the government continues to have an impact on the production of goods and services despite privatization. Since standard indicators of the government's withdrawal from economic decision-making are potentially misleading, the following attempts to document in a qualitative manner the shortcomings of the government's public policies.

---

[142] See IMF (1998.2).

Table 7.1. Jamaica: Selected Economic Indicators

	62-98	62-73	73-98	73-80	81-90	91-98	96	97	98
Real GDP growth	1.8	5.8	0.2	-2.4	2.5	-0.1	-1.9	-2.4	-0.7
Inflation (period average)	17.1	4.9	22.7	21.8	15.1	31.3	26.4	9.7	8.7
Current account									
(in percent of GDP) 1/	n.a.	n.a.	-5.2	-3.9	-7.5	-2.9	-2.5	-5.4	-4.4
Fiscal balance									
(in percent of GDP) 2/	n.a.	n.a.	-4.4	-18.8	-4.8	-0.7	-6.8	-8.9	-7.5

Sources: IMF. International Finance Statistics; Planning Institute of Jamaica; Economic and Social Survey Jamaica.

1/ Current account in U.S. dollars times average exchange rate. Averages cover the period 1976-98 only.

2/ Fiscal year balances as a percent of calendar year GDP. Averages cover the period 1979-98 only and refer to central government.

7.2.1   Continued government involvement

First, while the government has divested many public entities, in 1997 the government continued to have either full or partial ownership in 133 public entities.[143] While some of the entities fulfill traditional public service functions and are not likely to be privatized, the scope for divestment and hence for potential increases in efficiency is still large. These entities include, for example, large companies such as the local petroleum refinery (Petrojam), the electric utility (JPSCO), the country's water company (National Water Commission), as well as holdings of hotels, distilleries, and shares in the national airline carrier (AirJamaica).

Second, even though Jamaica privatized a number of export industries, it still continues to influence the behavior of many of the key export industries through marketing boards. In the past many developing countries such as Jamaica relied on industry or marketing boards as a means of fixing producer prices for export products. Such government intervention was justified on the grounds that it would protect domestic producers from fluctuations in world market prices and

---

[143] See IMF (1998.2).

exploitation by monopsonist exporters. Since export prices in domestic currency depend on the world market price of the particular product and the exchange rate, a producer price that is fixed by a marketing board could produce either additional revenue for government coffers or an additional fiscal burden. However, since many boards tended to operate in a rather asymmetric fashion, providing resources at a time of low prices but not leading to additional revenues for the government at a time of higher prices, market boards tended to be a drain on the budget. While in many countries marketing boards have been abolished, the Jamaican government continues to own industry and marketing boards such as the Coffee Industry Board, the Banana Board, The Cocoa Industry Board, the Coconut Industry Board, the Sugar Industry Authority, the Agricultural Marketing Board, and the Jamaica Tourist Board. As will be shown below in the case of the coffee board, the existence of such boards has prevented the privatized and deregulated industries from facing hard budget constraints. The mere transfer of ownership does not automatically change the behavior and improve the productive efficiency of these enterprises.

Third, despite privatization and liberalization, Jamaica continues to pursue an active industrial policy and to pick "winners and losers" through various means including a system of direct incentive schemes and subsidized and directed credits. The country's industrial policy is laid out in its National Industrial Policy Plan, the goal of which is to reach economic growth of 6 percent per year in order to double the current level of income per capita by the year 2010. The program states, for example, that:

The strategic focus of the Policy is (a) export push, through building and sustaining targeted areas of competitive advantage in the national economy, and (b) efficient import substitution, consistent with the focus on international competitiveness as the key element of the policy. ... By selective interventions and targeted allocations of taxes and expenditure, the Government seeks to create conditions at both the macroeconomic and microeconomic levels, which serve to facilitate and stimulate investment in the economy. ... Industrial Policy is based on the positive commitment to a market-driven economy. But it is not a policy of 'development by invitation'. It is an activist policy geared to ensuring growth and development of the productive base of the Jamaican economy by adoption of focused policy interventions in an active partnership between the state and private sector (Government of Jamaica. 1996: 4-5).

The industrial policy plan confirms that while Jamaica divested public entities over the years, the government continues to play an activist role in the economy. As a matter of fact, Gladstone (1998) estimates that the support to the productive sector, including hotels, from tax incentives alone reached Jamaica dollar 7 billion (3.2 percent of GDP) and increased by more than 80 percent between 1992 and 1996. Besides directing economic activity through an elaborate system of tax incentive schemes, the government provides direct lending at below market interest rates as well as equity support through various public institutions such as the National Development Bank of Jamaica, the National Investment Bank of Jamaica, the Agricultural Development Bank and the Export-Import Bank. The emphasis on subsidized and directed credit as a means of stimulating economic activity has increased rather than decreased over the last couple of years.[144]

Fourth, the government exhibits a willingness and tendency to provide support to loss-making privatized and other private entities. The evidence that the government has supported major businesses that are faced with bankruptcy is overwhelming. Such intervention has occurred in the form of direct support, the assumption of contingent liabilities, and the assumption of private sector debt. The following examples demonstrate how the government has failed to impose a hard budget constraint on privatized entities and how this has affected the behavior of the companies.

7.2.1.1   Air Jamaica

The national airline carrier AirJamaica was sold by the government to the Air Jamaica Acquisition Group in 1994. In line with most Jamaican privatizations, the airline was sold to domestic investors to ensure that the company would remain in the hands of Jamaicans. This bias toward national investors prevented international airline carriers with adequate financial resources and industry experience from assuming ownership. Since divestment, the airline is estimated to have run losses of some U.S. dollar 140 million (2 percent of 1997 GDP).[145] Attempts by a former chief executive officer to streamline the company and to return it to profitability by reducing employment, cutting services, and reducing the number of planes ended with the dismissal of the CEO.[146]

While a privately operated company faced with a hard budget would have had to increase efficiency to survive, AirJamaica has been able to rely on the government both for subsidies and the assumption of risk. In order to keep the company afloat, the government initially acquired non-voting preferential shares, and provided letters of comfort and government guarantees as well as direct cash injections.[147] As of late, it assumed U.S. dollar 115 million in liabilities that it had previously guaranteed. Despite the large support the company has received so far, the airline claims that some additional U.S. dollar 135 million in government-backed loans will be needed through the year 2000. In turn, the government has pledged publicly to provide the funds needed to keep the national airline carrier alive. The minister of finance has been paraphrased in the Gleaner as saying that:

... while not issuing a 'blank cheque', Air Jamaica chairman, Gordon 'Butch' Steward could be assured that the support would be continued as he did not want Jamaica to be in the position of the Eastern Caribbean islands, which, 'to put it euphemistically, have been put under pressure by virtue of their reliance on an external airline (The Gleaner, April 9, 1999).

---

[144] See, for example, Ministry of Finance (1998).

[145] See The Financial Gleaner, January 23, 1998.

[146] See Insight, March 21, 1998.

[147] See The Gleaner, January 30, 1998; and The Gleaner, April 21, 1998.

Unlike in the case of a public entity, the government provides the support but has not acquired any control in the company to stop the financial hemorrhage, inviting rent-seeking behavior. A call for the takeover of the airline by the government will only be a function of time.

7.2.1.2   Sugar Company of Jamaica

Another example of a privatization failure is Jamaica's sugar industry. Sugar is one of Jamaica's traditional export commodities, accounting on average for about 7 percent of goods exports during the period FY1993/94 through FY1997/98 and employing about 19 percent of the agricultural labor force.[148] The largest sugar company, the Sugar Company of Jamaica (SCJ), was sold to the private sector in 1993/94 for a sales price of Jamaica dollar 1.2 billion (1.1 percent of GDP). As in the airline case, the company was sold to domestic investors lacking the financial resources to ensure the viability of the company. Not only did the buyers lack the funds to undertake the necessary capital investment, but in addition they had to rely on government loans to finance the initial purchase. Even in 1997 the buyers continued to owe the government about 50 percent of the sales price plus accrued interest.

The government made public that the rationale for divesting the entity was to (a) increase efficiency, (b) reduce the fiscal burden, (c) broaden ownership, and (d) gain access to new markets.[149] However, the very behavior of the government has prevented the enterprise from achieving the stated objectives. In addition to the prevention of foreign ownership which would have assured access to capital and managerial know-how, the government has continued to bail out the company. As a result of the huge losses since privatization and despite the fact that Jamaica enjoys preferential access for sugar to the European Market under the Lomé agreement, the government has provided support to the company of U.S. dollar 100 million.[150] In addition to failing to change the incentive structure of the company by imposing a hard budget constraint, government intervention has delayed improvements in the company's profitability by taking explicit steps to minimize workforce reductions. This was done despite the fact that production costs in Jamaica are almost twice as high as world market prices.[151]

Instead, and in order to avoid a strike in a private company, the government brokered an agreement during the FY 1998 wage negotiations between the unions, the sugar producers' federations and the government allowing workers to realize sizable real wage increases. Since the employers were reluctant to provide real wage increases, the government even agreed to finance part of the wage increase.

---

[148] See IMF (1998.2) and The Financial Gleaner, July 25, 1997.

[149] See The Financial Gleaner, January 23, 1998.

[150] A small portion of the U.S. dollar 100 million were earmarked for the smaller Tropicana Company.

[151] See Insight, November 1996.

According to the agreement—which covers a period of two years—workers receive nominal wage increases of 10 percent in the first year and another 10 percent in the following year.[152] The government agreed to finance 25 percent and 50 percent respectively.[153] The above stated shows that while the company was formally in the hands of the private sector, it never operated as a private entity but rather as a public company that maintained its function as an employer of last resort. It also demonstrates that the government never took its own stated goals for privatizing SCJ seriously. Faced with more demands on the fiscal coffers, the government "re-nationalized" SCJ in the second half of 1998, some 6 years after it was first privatized. According to estimates, liabilities of the SCJ exceeded assets by about U.S. dollar 70 million.[154]

7.2.1.3   Coffee Industry Board (CIB)

Among agricultural products, coffee is Jamaica's second most important export commodity next to bananas, accounting for almost 40 percent of agricultural exports and 2 percent of total goods exports. While a portion of coffee production was liberalized and privatized, Jamaica's coffee board has remained a public entity and operates both as a commercial entity with its own coffee farms and as a regulator.[155] With the exception of the larger deregulated farmers, the board has the sole right to buy, process and sell coffee abroad. A report for the agricultural ministry that became public in 1997 reveals how CIB perpetuates the inefficiencies in the coffee industry and contributes to the fiscal burden of the government.[156] As a public entity, the board has been able to access funds from abroad with government guarantees. While the funds have been used to finance its own operations, CIB has also provided loans to large private coffee farmers. However, unlike traditional finance institutions, CIB has signaled to its borrowers that it does not enforce collection. This attitude is reflected in a statement by the president of CIB, who was quoted in the Sunday Observer: "We don't, for example, foreclose on people when they don't pay their loan. We tend to empathise with them when crops fail and they aren't able to service their debt." (The Sunday Observer, April 6, 1997). Under such circumstances, even though coffee farmers are operating as private entities, they lack incentives to streamline their operations and to improve efficiency. As in most cases, the government justifies its actions by explaining that it cannot let a key industry go bankrupt. In the case of the coffee industry, the minister of agriculture indicated in the bailout of the Jablum coffee company that the Blue Mountain

---

[152] Real wage increases were about 2 percent in FY1998/99 and are estimated to be about 4 percent in FY 1999/00, based on an inflation target of 6 percent.

[153] See The Gleaner, April 21, 1998.

[154] See The Gleaner, October 28, 1998.

[155] Part of the shortcomings of the CIB are related to the structure of its board. While CIB is a public entity, a large number of the nine board members are coffee farmers themselves, causing a conflict of interest. See The Sunday Observer (1997).

[156] See Insight, June 1, 1997.

coffee is "our Rolls Royce industry and we can't allow it to die on the vine". (Sunday Herald, June 22, 1997). In 1999, CIB announced that it was insolvent and called on the government to assume its debts. Given that its liabilities exceeded its assets by Jamaica dollar 1 billion (U.S. 27 million) and that most of CIB's debt is government guaranteed, the Jamaican taxpayer will have to pay for the inefficiencies.[157]

While most indicators suggest that the structure of the economy has changed substantially over the past two decades and led to a retreat of government ownership and intervention, the above examples indicate that government retrenchment has been limited and the presence of the public sector continues to be overwhelming. While many more companies are in private hands than in the 1970s and early 1980s, the government continues to bail out major industries that are faced with financial difficulties. In addition to the ones mentioned, over the past couple of years the government has bailed out other key industries in distress such as the garment and citrus industries and the JTA housing cooperative[158]. The government's pervasiveness and willingness to bail out insolvent industries and to re-assume ownership became even more apparent in the context of the FY 1996/97 financial crisis.

7.2.2   Government involvement in the financial sector

The extension of the government's involvement in the economy in the 1970s was not only limited to the ownership of productive entities but included the allocation of savings through commercial banks such as Workers Bank[159] as well as development banks such as the Agricultural Development Bank and the Jamaica Development Bank. In addition, the government had nationalized key financial institutions such as the largest domestic commercial bank (National Commercial Bank, NCB), which was purchased by the government from Barclays Bank International in 1977.[160] In line with the government's new policy of divesting productive entities in the mid 1980s, it also began to divest financial institutions. For example, NCB was sold to the private sector in several tranches starting in 1986 and Workers Savings and Loan Bank was divested in 1991. As in the case of productive assets, the acquisition of ownership was largely limited to domestic investors. However, while the government privatized and liberalized the financial sector, little attention was paid to the establishment of an effective regulatory framework, casting doubt on the seriousness of the government's commitment to improving economic efficiency. Certain sectors of the financial system, such as building societies, remained almost entirely unregulated. Even in sectors that were

---

[157] See The Gleaner, May 13, 1999.

[158] The Weekend Observer, February, 7, 1997. Shake-up at JTA Housing Co-op.

[159] Workers Bank is a partly owned government entity which was formed out of the Government Savings Bank in 1973.

[160] For an overview of Jamaica's financial system see Lue Lim (1991).

eventually formally regulated, such as the insurance industry, regulation remained largely ineffective. On the one hand, the Insurance Act that was passed in 1992 did not include solvency assessments, and on the other hand the government failed even to appoint the Superintendent of Insurance. Furthermore, in mid-1997 when the financial sector crisis was already fully under way, the agency still lacked qualified staff to carry out on-site inspections.[161]

7.2.2.1   Causes and responses by the government to the financial sector crisis

During the period of liberalization and privatization, the financial sector expanded rapidly and the number of financial institutions mushroomed. For example, the number of commercial banks increased from 8 to 11 between 1981 and 1995, while the number of merchant banks increased from 6 to 25 and building societies from 7 to 15 respectively. The growth was the largest in sectors that were the least regulated and faced the lowest taxes. In order to avoid regulation and implicit taxes such as non-remunerated cash reserve requirements, financial conglomerates established specialized banks as a means of increasing their deposit base and accessing cheap funds. In the end, such conglomerates comprised a commercial bank, a merchant bank, an investment bank, a building society and an insurance company. As a result of the weak regulatory framework, the distinction between deposit-taking and other financial institutions became blurred, leading to a mismatch of maturities between assets and liabilities and encouraging lending to connected parties. The financial system's ability to perform its traditional function of channeling savings to their most productive use deteriorated over time. Instead resources were often allocated based on connections and political considerations. In 1996 the Jamaica minister of commerce pointed out that "... [a]t the end of June this year, commercial banks either invested, loaned or gave guarantee for loans to connecting parties amounting to Jamaica dollar 11.28 billion ....". (The Gleaner, November, 1996.). Furthermore, as the closure of one of the local banks revealed, even the former prime minister and current leader of the opposition, Edward Seaga, was a beneficiary of the system since a loan amounting to U.S. dollar 2 million was one of the outstanding non-performing loans.[162]

The weakness of the financial system became apparent to the public in 1994 with the failure of a small financial institution, the Blaise Group. Despite the weakness of the system, the government engaged in a drastic anti-inflationary effort at the end of 1995 in order to bring inflation down to that of its trading partners. The unbalanced combination of a tight monetary policy and a relaxed fiscal policy brought the weakness of Jamaica's financial system fully to the fore. Rising real interest rates and the policy-induced recession led to liquidity and solvency problems in the financial system.

After the minister of finance intervened in one of the institutions (Century) and after two bank runs (Citizens Bank and Eagle Bank), the government opted to state

---

[161] See The Gleaner, July 24, 1997.

[162] See EIU (1996).

publicly that it would effectively bail out all institutions. Despite the fact that the government did not have a deposit insurance scheme in place, it announced that it would guarantee all depositors, life insurance holders, and pensioners. Institutionally, it established a new public entity, the Financial Sector Adjustment Company (FINSAC) as a means of pursuing multiple objectives including liquidity and capital support, the restructuring of financial entities, and the divestment of those that had been acquired. As a public agency, FINSAC can issue instruments to provide capital support that are guaranteed by the government.

7.2.2.2   Cost and implications of the financial sector bailout

According to government estimates, the bailout of the financial sector has resulted in the protection of some 1.5 million depositors and almost 600 thousand individual insurance policy holders. Furthermore, the fact that the government opted to bail out all institutions prevented a financial panic and a foreign exchange crisis. The gross fiscal cost, however, has been staggering. Support by FINSAC alone amounted to some Jamaica dollar 90 billion (36 percent of GDP) at the end of May 1999 and further support—both to provide liquidity and to continue the recapitalization—is likely to be necessary.[163] In terms of GDP, the gross fiscal cost already exceeds that of countries which have been major recipients of government support as a result of a financial sector crisis. For example, the rescue of the Venezuelan financial sector amounted to 17 percent of GDP, the cost of the Mexican bailout amounted to around 6.5 percent of GDP, and the fiscal cost of the failure of the savings-and-loan associations in the U.S. is estimated at 2.6 percent of GDP.[164]

The willingness to provide a blanket guarantee and to bail out all financial institutions is consistent with the government's behavior in the productive sector of the economy. The government's continued assumption of risk will prevent the private sector firms from operating as true private institutions. The adverse implications of the government's strategy are multifold and are likely to dampen the growth potential of the economy for years to come. The increase in public liabilities as a result of the financial sector bailout will increase interest payments by the government and hence imply higher taxes for current and future generations. Higher income taxes will undermine work effort, while regressive consumption-based taxes will increase poverty, leading to more violence and social unrest.[165] Furthermore,

---

[163] See The Gleaner, June 18, 1999. The cost excludes, for example, support provided by Financial Institutions Services (FIS) in the context of the liquidation of the Blaise Financial Group and the Century Financial Entities, amounting to about Jamaica dollar 12 billion (4.5 percent of GDP).

[164] On financial sector support see Lindgren, Garica, Saal (1996): 76-77.

[165] The potential implications of tax increases became apparent in the aftermath of a gasoline tax hike. After the government announced a substantial increase in gasoline taxes in the context of its FY 1999/00 budget, massive protests and street violence took place, adversely affecting the tourism sector. The government opted to withdraw its tax increase. See The Gleaner, April 20, 1999.

given the added default risk of the government as a result of the increase in the debt stock, interest rates are likely to stay high, undermining private sector investments. Although the provision of capital support was accompanied by the acquisition of full or partial ownership in some 158 entities, reducing the gross liabilities of the public sector, as the assets are divested again the net liabilities are likely to exceed 50 percent of the support that has been provided. The degree to which FINSAC's liabilities exceed its assets became apparent when the institution wrote down a large percentage of its assets.

Besides the government's strategy of guaranteeing all depositors and insurance policy holders, the magnitude of the support is to some degree related to the fact that FINSAC had to rely on negotiations in order to acquire ownership stakes in return for capital and liquidity support.[166] During the negotiations, owners and managers of financial institutions had the opportunity to draw out the process, causing the financial institutions to hemorrhage even further and inviting rent-seeking behavior through asset stripping and the continued payment of large salaries to management. The magnitude of the cost was aided by a lack of public debate about the government's approach to rescuing the financial system. The fact that FINSAC operates as an extrabudgetary fund and issues government-guaranteed instruments without prior budgetary approval contributes to a lack of public accountability.[167] This was, for example, expressed by the head of the Jamaican Chamber of Commerce, who pointed out that:

Without this kind of disclosure, we can never have public accountability. And without such accountability and a disciplined approach to controlling public expenditure, we are condemning ourselves to a cycle of mismanagement, economic retardation and persistent poverty for our people (The Gleaner, May 19, 1999).

In addition, the bailout of the financial sector implied that the government has assumed control or ownership of the domestic banking system—excluding one small institution (Trafalgar Bank) but including those that had previously been privatized—and about 90 percent of the life insurance industry.[168] The government's bailout strategy also resulted in the acquisition of real assets in other sectors of the economy that were in the portfolio of institutions in which FINSAC intervened. For example, the government acquired 10 hotels, among other real estate.[169] Since FINSAC is charged with numerous mandates, including the acquisition, restructuring and eventual privatization of financial entities, it is

---

[166] This contrasts, for example, with the Resolution Trust Company that was established in the context of the savings-and-loan debacle in the U.S. which had the legal powers to intervene.

[167] The FY1999/00 budget makes provisions though for additional liquidity support for FINSAC institutions.

[168] See Chen-Young (1998).

[169] See IMF (1998).

questionable whether FINSAC will cease to exist any time soon or will remain the largest public holding company in the country for many years to come.[170]

As a result of the de facto "renationalization" of the domestic financial system, the assumption of private sector commercial entities, the increased provision of subsidized and directed lending and incentive schemes, and the widespread custom of bailing out inefficient entities, the presence of the government in the economy is similar to or even greater than during the heyday of the 1970s. To some degree such a hypothesis is even confirmed by the minister of finance, who stated that:

... several other significant divestments have failed and in certain instances, the State's involvement in post-divestment, in terms of its commitment of resources is even greater than before divestment took place, indicating that the losses racked up at operations such as National Commercial Bank, Caribbean Cement Company, the sugar estates as well as Air Jamaica and the hotels, which were divested in the 1970s, have continued to be a drain on the public purse (The Gleaner, September 25, 1998).

In effect, Jamaica has come full circle, reverting to an economic structure similar to that preceding the process of privatization and liberalization. Besides illustrating the direct cost of such policies, Jamaica's example solidifies the general perception that governments that bear the risk of failing private enterprises encourage moral hazard.

7.3   Jamaica's political system and half-hearted reforms

Governments that engage in economic reforms to improve the growth potential of the economy should undertake privatization in a way that is consistent with this objective. In particular, such a government would use efficient and transparent privatization methods that minimize insider transactions and maximize the probability of attracting investors that can generate the highest return, irrespective of whether the buyers are domestic or foreign investors. Furthermore, it would establish a regulatory framework to minimize allocative inefficiency in monopolistic markets. Given the importance of a stable and efficient financial system for the allocation of funds and the potential for rent-seeking behavior, the privatization of financial institutions would go hand-in-hand with the establishment of regulatory and supervisory agencies.

However, governments that use privatization for opportunistic purposes may be inclined to implement privatization programs that are inconsistent with improving efficiency and growth. For example, although the government formally divests its productive assets, it may continue to influence decision-making in the private sector directly or through its actions. As long as the government fails to impose a hard budget constraint on privatized entities, the behavior of such companies is not likely to change. In addition, politicians that engage in privatization for opportunistic reasons will probably abandon their policy of divestment more readily. It would not

---

[170] At the time of its establishment it was envisioned that FINSAC would wind down its operations after to 5 to 7 years. See Bonnick (1997).

be inconceivable to see the very same government and political party that once embraced privatization turn around and call for more government intervention and even re-nationalization. The above-listed evidence for Jamaica strongly suggests that both political parties had only limited commitment to allowing the market to allocate resources and provide goods and services. The following intends to establish that both parties used privatization as a means of either pleasing international financial institutions or transferring private resources to their respective political constituencies.

Jamaica's political system has been dominated by two parties: the People's National Party (PNP) and the Jamaica Labor Party (JLP).[171] Ideologically, the JNP has been associated with being more "left wing"—at times with socialist tendencies—whereas the JLP is considered to be more "right wing". However, despite official party platforms, the differences between the two parties and their respective constituencies are less clearcut. Jamaica's political party system is relatively unique in that both parties have close ties to trade unions.[172] Even the more "right wing" JLP is directly related to the labor movement and an offspring of the Bustamente Industrial Trade Union (BITU). Hence, the traditional distinction between one party that reflects the interest of labor and another that relies on owners of capital, with the former generally less supportive of privatization, does not hold in the case of Jamaica. Indeed, the actual positions of the two parties with respect to the economic role of the private sector have changed repeatedly over the years. For example, whereas the JLP has tended to rely more on market solutions than their PNP counterpart, JLP policies in the 1960s embraced protectionism as a means of achieving rapid industrialization. As a matter of fact, Danielson and Lundahl (1994) point out that both parties pursued policies in the 1960s and 1970s that were fairly similar.[173] While the more "right wing" JLP was not at odds with government intervention in the 1960s and 1970s, the former socialist PNP had officially come around and started to embrace privatization and a market-based approach at the end of the 1980s. The late Michael Manley, in his first term as PNP prime minister in the 1970s, advocated the nationalization of key sectors of the economy and expanded the role of the public sector; during his second tenure as prime minister which began in 1988, he continued at least formally with the economic reforms, including privatization, that had previously been instituted by the opposition party. The view that the differences between the two parties are rather marginal was even expressed by the current minister of finance from the PNP, who stated that "To a large extent the period 1986 to the present, although

---

[171] Although a split by the JLP resulted in the establishment of a third party—the National Democratic Party— the influence of the third party has been marginal. The NDP is not represented in Parliament.

[172] The JLP is associated with the Bustamente Industrial Trade Union whereas the PNP receives its support from the National Workers Union.

[173] See Danielson and Lundahl (1994).

covering two political regimes, has been marked by a continuation of economic policies." (Davies, 1991: 6)[174]

The fact that both parties might have embraced privatization for opportunistic reasons is reflected on the one hand in the way privatization was implemented over the last decade. Despite the large number of companies that were sold to the private sector, almost all companies were sold to domestic buyers, inviting rent-seeking behavior and favoritism.[175] One of the few companies that were sold to a foreign investor was sold in a way that is clearly at odds with creating an environment for growth and improved efficiency. The purchase of the Jamaican telephone company by Cable and Wireless provides the operator with outright monopoly rights for all telecommunications services. The monopoly position covers all domestic services, including cellular phones, international link-ups, and the telephone infrastructure, through the year 2004. Monopoly rights for international services—excluding satellite services—are even guaranteed until the year 2013.[176] Unless the government is able to renegotiate some of the terms, the monopoly position in such a key industry is likely to affect investment and growth adversely. Similarly, the liberalization and privatization of financial institutions was implemented without adequate emphasis on the establishment and staffing of regulatory and supervisory institutions.

On the other hand, both political parties have been readily willing to abandon their privatization efforts. In the case of the JLP opposition party this is reflected in its latest rhetoric, and in the case of the governing party through its actual policies of continued government intervention and the re-nationalization of many of the privatized entities. For example, the current leader of the opposition party, who as Jamaica's prime minister spearheaded the privatization wave in the mid-1980s, has called publicly on the government to stop all privatizations. During the 1996 election campaign, he threatened to re-nationalize the electric utility JPSCO if the government went ahead with its plan of selling the company to one of the two final bidders.[177] In line with opportunistic behavior, the opposition party was concerned that the sale of JPSCO would allow the governing party to use the sales proceeds of U.S. dollar 111 million or U.S. dollar 160 million, depending on which bidder was accepted, as a means of financing the election campaign or buying out particular voting groups.[178] The opposition party justified its call for continued government involvement in the electricity sector by reverting to a rhetoric that can hardly be

---

[174] The same view is expressed by the United States Foreign Service. See United States Foreign Service (1998).

[175] Stone (1991) points out that in the case of the privatization of 15 hotels between 1981 and 1990 only one was outright sold to a foreign investor.

[176] See United States Foreign Service (1998).

[177] The privatization had been advanced to the point where a final cabinet decision had to be made to accept one of the two final and U.S. based bidders—Southern Electric or Houston Industries. In the end, the government rejected both bids and postponed the privatization indefinitely.

[178] See The Gleaner, November 6, 1996.

squared with commitment to a liberalized and privately run economy. The spokesperson of the JLP for public utilities stated, for example, that:

While the JLP welcomes foreign investment, JLP policy required that essential services such as JPSCo. be nationally held and controlled in order to ensure that the pace of development be determined by the overall economic and social needs of the country and not solely by the ideological dictates of liberalization (The Gleaner, October 15, 1996).

In many respects the rhetoric was reminiscent of that used in the 1960s and 1970s to justify government ownership. Furthermore, the JLP party also called on the government to pick "winners and losers" by providing targeted sectors with financial support to stimulate economic growth.[179]

It appears that both parties, when in power, have used privatization as a means of addressing short-term macroeconomic imbalances such as balance-of-payments or fiscal crises and of accessing funds and receiving the stamp of approval from the international financial community. The following statement from the current PNP minister of finance reflects the fact that the respective governments never considered themselves to be the architects of the reform programs, undermining their effectiveness from the outset.

Apart from external factors, the Jamaican economy, especially in the last 15 years or so, has been affected by the policy dictates of the major international financial institutions from which we borrow, as well as by those of our major bilateral creditors. Whilst it is impossible to establish definitive dates to mark the beginning of particular periods of influence, there can be no doubt that the decade of the 1980s, dominated by the trans-Atlantic Reagan-Thatcher alliance, was such a period. Their leadership, and the policies which they articulated, did not only dominate their domestic agendas but also had a profound influence on the policies of international financial institutions. Whilst these institutions had always explicitly supported the primacy of the market in the allocation of resources, they became increasingly aggressive in their policy demands (Davies, 1994:7).

Furthermore, the Gleaner writes that the minister stated that "... he (minister of finance) went a step further in blaming the IMF for many of the problems we are facing now, for forcing the Government into deregulation". (The Financial Gleaner, April 11, 1997).

7.4   Summary

Despite Jamaica's economic reform programs that started in the mid-1980s and included a substantial reduction in the size of the public sector, the economy continues to be in the doldrums. The apparent change in the government's role is reflected in a number of indicators, such as the number of entities owned by the government, public sector employment, and the share of government output in overall economic activity.

---

[179] See The Gleaner, September 24, 1997

A closer analysis, however, suggests that the government continues to be omnipresent in the economy and that even enterprises that had been transferred to the private sector continue to rely on the government for financial support. Besides providing subsidies through incentive schemes and direct support, the government continues to assume the downward risk of private sector enterprises even to the extent of preventing business failures, as reflected in the provision of guarantees for enterprises such as AirJamaica or the "renationalization" of the Sugar Company of Jamaica. By doing so, the government effectively privatized the profits but continues to bear the losses.

The failure to enforce a hard budget constraint implies that privatized enterprises lack the incentive to improve their operational efficiency. The willingness of the government to bear the cost of inefficiently run entities is also reflected in the government's bailout of the entire domestic banking system in the aftermath of the 1996 financial crisis. As a result, Jamaican taxpayers assumed a liability that will continue to have adverse implications for years to come. In addition to the debt, the government runs the risk of rewarding rent-seeking behavior and distorting the risk/reward system of the private sector.

The fact that privatization has not led to an improvement in the country's economic conditions seems to be at least partially related to the fact that the reforms were implemented at best half-heartedly. Governments of both political parties have demonstrated through their actions and rhetoric that their commitment to a market-based allocation of resources and less government is limited. While in power, the JLP limited the sale of assets to largely domestic investors, continues to fight foreign investments as shown by the case of the electric utility JPSCO, and called on the current government to stop privatization. The party currently in office, PNP, in turn has failed to enforce hard budget constraints, continues to emphasize the role of the government in fostering growth as reflected in its industrial policy, and has de facto renationalized most entities that were once privatized. It appears that economic reform measures such as liberalization and privatization were chosen as a means of addressing macroeconomic imbalances in the short term and of accessing funds from international financial institutions. As a result of the failure to embrace reform, Jamaica has come full circle and levels of government ownership and intervention are again similar to those in the 1970s.

8 Summary and Conclusion

Ever since Britain began its large-scale privatization program in the early 1980s, the world has experienced a change in paradigm that has allowed governments to use privatization as an instrument of public policy. By now, most governments have taken advantage of this new instrument and have divested or are currently in the process of divesting a large portion of their public assets.

The potential gains in terms of increases in efficiency, living standards, and long run growth potential are substantial in many countries. Most empirical studies show that countries that protect private property rights and rely on the private sector to produce goods and services have a better track record in terms of their growth performance than those that rely heavily on the public sector.

Besides a one-time improvement in output as a result of the reallocation of resources in the aftermath of privatization, divestment can potentially also affect the national savings rate and the long run growth rate of the economy. Increases in the national savings rate are, however, related more to the political willingness of the government to cut benefits and reduce transfer payments than to the privatization of public entities. The same argument applies to the privatization of pay-as-you-go social security systems. The privatization of the Chilean social security system, for example, has reportedly affected national savings only indirectly through a deepening of capital markets. In terms of the profitability of privatized enterprises, a number of studies suggest that the operational performance of public enterprises improves once they are transferred to the private sector. However, to infer from an improved performance on the enterprise level that the economy has moved closer to the production possibility frontier is premature. Besides the fact that the enterprises earmarked for privatization are not a random sample but are likely to reflect a selection bias by governments toward those that will become "success stories", a number of studies remain inconclusive or even show a deterioration in the performance of the privatized enterprises. The relatively poor performance of publicly traded privatized European companies suggests that the restructuring of the enterprises is not advancing as rapidly as expected.

The study raised the question of whether it is prudent to assume that governments are driven primarily by efficiency considerations in their initial decision to divest public assets. The political economy literature suggests otherwise. Governments in elected democracies have in the past all too often pursued objectives that did not coincide with the maximization of social welfare. The political economy literature argues that, driven by such objectives as winning re-election or rewarding special interest groups with particular macroeconomic outcomes, governments have tended to delay reforms, embark on economic policies that are unsustainable in the long term, and generate politically motivated business cycles. The political advantages of using privatization as a means of delaying economic reforms or affecting macroeconomic aggregates in a predetermined fashion were quantitatively demonstrated using a simple macroeconomic framework.

If policymakers have embarked on the sale of assets because of a change in their behavior and have learnt as a result of past mistakes, privatization failures may be attributed to shortcomings in the design and implementation of the privatization programs. Better advice could remedy these shortcomings in the case of ongoing or future divestments. However, the conclusions differ substantially if governments have engaged in privatization for reasons that are not compatible with increasing the growth potential of the economy.

Indeed, the study argues that other objectives have often been the driving force behind divestment and have contributed to the current privatization frenzy. The single most important one is related to fiscal issues. While it may not be controversial to argue that cash-strapped governments faced with a hard budget constraint resort to the sale of assets as a means of financing, this argument is more applicable to developing countries than to industrialized countries with developed capital markets. However, even in the United States and many western European countries, fiscal issues seem to be a key determinant of privatization. While industrialized countries have an efficient tax system, a broad tax base and almost unlimited access to domestic and foreign financing, it appears that the financing of government expenditure through the sale of assets encounters the least political resistance. Alternatively, governments that maintain a given level of expenditure but reduce the publicly visible deficit through privatization may be politically rewarded. This phenomenon became quite apparent in the run-up to European Monetary Union. Even countries such as Germany engaged in creative accounting practices through the sale of assets to convince the general public and capital markets of their tough fiscal policies and to meet the Maastricht criteria. While doing so was perceived to be politically opportune, some of the real fiscal adjustments have merely been postponed to future years and it remains to be seen— given the overarching fiscal objectives— whether the transfer of ownership to the public sector will indeed lead to an improvement in efficiency.

If one were to rank the different forms of financing in terms of the actual or perceived resistance by voters, governments would be least likely to raise taxes and would prefer the sale of assets to increases in the publicly visible deficit. Irrespective of whether one assumes that voters are myopic or rational, the tendency of the public to be indifferent to the sale of assets can probably be explained by the lack of transparency of most privatization transactions in terms of their fiscal implications.

Other potential key determinants of privatization are related to balance-of-payments crises and monetary policy. The study argued that the sheer size of some of the privatization programs can pose a challenge to conducting monetary policy—especially in countries with underdeveloped capital markets—but can also serve as an additional instrument for dealing with temporary surges in capital inflows. Countries such as Argentina have supported their anti-inflationary programs by using privatization receipts as a partial substitute for monetization of fiscal deficits. As the section on balance-of-payments issues showed, the recent financial crisis in South East Asia prompted governments that previously limited foreign ownership in public enterprises and financial institutions to change their policy direction and to promote the sale of public assets abroad. The "exceptional financing" characteristic of privatization in the aftermath of a balance-of-payments crisis suggests that governments may be willing to sacrifice efficiency considerations in order to ensure a maximum inflow of foreign exchange.

The frequently reported level of overstaffing in public enterprises suggests that profit-driven private investors who are free to reduce the labor force are likely to do so. The lack of wage flexibility and the rigidities and imperfections of labor markets imply that divestment is associated with at least temporarily if not permanently higher unemployment rates. The evidence that privatization is associated with a reduction in the workforce is supported by numerous studies at the enterprise level. A cursory review of unemployment rates before, during, and after privatization even suggests that unemployment rates tend to be higher during the year of privatization as well as in the following year. Governments that are faced by recurring elections have an incentive to minimize the political cost of creating unemployment. Besides subjecting new investors to employment commitments and other means of limiting the employment impact of privatization, governments tend to reduce the political opposition by making generous retrenchment and severance payments. The case study on Pakistan confirms that the fiscal costs of such generous transfer payments can be very large, adversely affecting the macroeconomy.

Countries that exploit privatization for short-term political reasons run the risk that divestment is not associated with tangible improvements in the structure of the economy and in the living conditions of the population. A disillusioned public might ultimately even call for renewed government intervention and the renationalization of the privatized industries. The case study on Jamaica provides some evidence of such a privatization failure. Successive governments seem to have exploited privatization to address short-term macroeconomic imbalances and to access foreign financing, including financing from international organizations. Given the lack of commitment to "real" economic reforms, the Jamaican government failed to implement hard budget constraints and prevented key industries from restructuring. Their failure to do so has contributed to the continued poor growth performance of the country and a de facto renationalization of major industries, including the financial sector.

The study suggests that, at all levels of economic development, governments frequently do not take their own publicly announced rationale for privatization—the desire to increase efficiency—seriously. The ability of governments to use privatization to pursue short-term political objectives that are inconsistent with an improvement in economic welfare is partly related to the lack of transparency of privatization-related transactions and the discretionary power of politicians. As in the case of other time-inconsistent behavior by governments, the establishment of clear policy rules can potentially reduce the exploitation of privatization for particular political objectives. Such rules would, as a minimum, commit governments to market-based privatization methods such as public auctions and transparent bidding processes. In case of the latter, the government should, for example, commit itself to accepting the highest bid offered once pre-announced minimum conditions are met. The less market-based the privatization process, the greater the chances for outright corruption and the transfer of wealth and income to special interest groups. Besides raising issues of equity, non-market-based privatizations can adversely affect the government's intertemporal budget constraint and, if sufficiently large, the macroeconomy as a whole. Privately negotiated divestments are especially prone to insider deals and to undervaluations favoring special interest groups.

In order to increase transparency and encourage public debate about the use of privatization receipts, the currently common practice of channeling the receipts from privatization through extrabudgetary funds should be eliminated. As the case study on Pakistan demonstrated, the use of extrabudgetary funds by governments invites the use of such receipts for political objectives. While the reliance, for example, on formal and transparent budget procedures does not eliminate the potential for the misuse of privatization receipts, institutional transparency increases the political cost of doing so. More transparency and hence accountability would also be ensured if governments were to move toward intergenerational accounting. This would ensure that the sale of assets is treated as analogous to an increase in government debt.

References

Abdala, Manuel Angel. 1994. Privatization and Changes in Welfare Costs of Inflation. *Journal of Public Economics* 55: 465-493.

Alesina, Alberto and Allan Drazen. 1991. Why are Stabilizations Delayed? *American Economic Review* 81.5: 1170-1188.

Alesina, Alberto and Howard Rosenthal. 1995. *Partisan Politics, Divided Government and the Economy*. Cambridge (University Press).

Alesina, Alberto and Nouriel Roubini. 1997. *Political Cycles and the Macroeconomy*. Cambridge, MA (MIT).

Alesina, Alberto and Summers, Lawrence. 1993. Central Bank Independence and Macroeconomic Performance. *Journal of Money, Credit and Banking* 25: 151-162.

Alesina, Alberto. 1987. Macroeconomic Policy in a Two-Party System as a Repeated Game. *Quarterly Journal of Economics* 102: 651-678.

Altonji, Joseph; Fumio Hayashi and Laurence J. Kotlikoff. 1992. Is the Extended Family Altruistically Linked? Direct Tests Using Micro Data. *American Economic Review* 82.5: 1177-98.

Arrow, Kenneth. 1985. The Economics of Agency. In J.W. Pratt and Richard Zeckhauser. Eds. *Principals and Agents: The Structure of Business*. Boston (Harvard Business School Press): 37-51.

Aschauer, David Alan and Jeremy Greenwood. 1985. Macroeconomic Effects of Fiscal Policy. Carnegie-Rochester Conference Series on Public Policy 23 (Autumn): 91-138.

Associated Press. 1995. The Belgian Government's Goal of Meeting Maastricht Treaty Criterion. Reported in IMF Morning News, January 26, 1995.

Azariadis, Costas. 1993. *Intertemporal Macroeconomics*. Cambridge, MA (Blackwell).

Aziz, Sartaj. 1996. *Privatisation in Pakistan*. Paris (OECD).

Bös, Dieter. 1991. *Privatization: A Theoretical Treatment*. New York (Oxford University Press).

Bös, Dieter and Gunter Kayser. 1995. The Last Days of the Treuhandanstalt. In Paul Cook and Colin Kirkpatrick. Eds. *Privatisation Policy and Performance*. New York (Prentice Hall): 84-100.

Baker, Mark. 1998. Introduction—Telecoms Offerings Dominate Record Year. In Mark Baker. Ed. *Privatisation International Yearbook*. London.

Baker, Mark. Ed. 1998. Privatisation International Yearbook. London (Privatisation International).

Baliño, J.T. Tomás and C. Enoch. 1997. Currency Board Arrangements: Issues and Experiences. *IMF Occasional Paper* 151. Washington, D.C. (IMF)

Banerji, Arup and Richard H. Sabot.1994. Wage Distortions, Overmanning, and Reform in Developing Country Public Enterprises. World Bank, Vice Presidency for Finance and Private Sector Development. Washington, D.C. (Photocopy).

Barro, Robert J. 1974. Are Government Bonds Net Wealth? *Journal of Political Economy* 82.6: 1095-1117.

Barro, Robert J. and Xavier Sala-i-Martin. 1995. *Economic Growth*. New York (McGraw-Hill).

Bernheim, Douglas. 1989. A Neoclassical Perspective on Budget Deficits. *Journal of Economic Perspectives* 3.2 (Spring): 55-72.

Bhaskar V. and Mushtaq Khan. 1995. Privatization and Employment: A Study of the Jute Industry in Bangladesh. *American Economic Review* 85.1: 267-73.

Bier, Willem. 1992. Macroeconomic Models for the PC. *IMF Working Paper* WP/92/110. Washington, D.C.

Bonnick, Gladstone. 1997. The Role, Functions and Achievements of FINSAC. Kingston (FINSAC). Photocopy.

Boyco, Maxim; Andrei Shleifer; and Robert W. Vishney (1994). A Theory of Privatization. *Harvard Institute for International Development Discussion Paper* 1689.

Brücker. Herbert. 1995. *Privatisierung in Ostdeutschland. Eine institutionenökonomische Analyse*. Frankfurt (Campus Verlag).

Brand, Christoph and Daniel Schmitz. 1996. Germany—Waiting for Telekom. In *Privatization Yearbook* 1996. Privatization International. London: 145-148.

Bruton, Henry. 1989. Import Substitution. In Holis Chenery and T. N. Eds. *Handbook in Development Economics*. Vol 2. Amsterdam (North-Holland): 1601-1644.

Buchanan, James M. and Richard E. Wagner. 1977. *Democracies in Deficit: The Political Legacy of Lord Keynes*. New York (Academic Press).

Buiter, Willem and James Tobin. 1979. Debt Neutrality: A Brief Review of Doctrine and Evidence. In George von Furstenberg. *Social Security versus Private Saving*. Cambridge, MA (Ballinger).

Bundesministerium der Finanzen. 1995. *Beteiligungsbericht* 1995. Bonn (Bundesanzeiger Verlagsgesellschaft).

Bundesministerium der Finanzen. Various Years. *Beteiligungsbericht*. Bonn (Bundesanzeiger Verlagsgesellschaft).

Calvo, Guillermo.1991. The Perils of Stabilization. *IMF Staff Papers* 38.4: 921-928.

Calvo, Guillermo; Leonardo Leiderman and Carmen M. Reinhard. 1993. Capital Inflows and Real Exchange Rate Appreciation in Latin America: The Role of External Factors. *IMF Staff Papers* 40.1: 108-150.

Case of ENTel Argentina. *Journal of Public Economics* 55: 465-493.

Cassel, Dieter. Ed. 1998. *50 Jahre Soziale Marktwirtschaft. Ordnungstheoretische Grundlagen, Realisierungsprobleme und Zukunftsperspektiven einer wirschaftspolitischen Konzeption*. Stuttgart (Lucius & Lucius).

CBO (Congressional Budget Office). 1989. Deficits and Interest Rates: Theoretical Issues and Simulation Results. *Staff Working Papers*. January: 5-12.

Chand, Sheetal K. and Albert Jaeger. 1996. Aging Populations and Public Pension Schemes. *IMF Occasional Paper* 147. Washington, D.C. (IMF).

Chen-Young, Paul. 1998. With All Good Intentions. The Collapse of Jamaica's Domestic Financial Sector. Center for Strategic and International Studies. *Policy Papers on the America* 9.12.

Cangiano, Marco, Carlo Cottarelli and Luis Cubeddu. 1998. Pension Developments and Reforms in Transition Economies. *IMF Working Paper* WP/98/151. Washington, D.C. (IMF).

Cox, Helmut. 1993. Öffentliche Unternehmen und Staatsbeteiligungen als Instrumente der Industriepolitik sowie strategischer Industrie- und Handelspolitik. *Diskussionsbeiträge zur öffentlichen Wirtschaft* 32. Duisburg University.

Cox, Helmut. 1994. Kommunale Sparkassen privatisieren? Bemerkungen aus ordnungs-und · wettbewerbstheoretischer Sicht. *Diskussionsbeiträge zur öffentlichen Wirtschaft* 33. Duisburg University.

Crafts, Nicholas. 1998. East Asian Growth Before and After the Crisis. *IMF Working Paper* WP/98/137. Washington, D.C.

Danielson, Anders and Mats Lundahl. 1994. Endogenous Policy Formation and the Principle of Optimal Obfuscation: Theory and Some Evidence from Haiti and Jamaica. *Comparative Economic Studies*. 36.3: 51-78.

Davies, Omar. 1994. The Jamaican Economy since Independence: Agenda for the Future. In Patsy Lewis.Ed.*Jamaica: Preparing for the Twenty-First Century*. Kingston (Ian Randle Publishing).

Deutsche Bank Research 1994. Kommunen unter Privatisierungsdruck. *Deutschland-Themen* 42 (November 8, 1994).

Diamond, Peter and Salvador Valdés. 1994. Social Security Reforms. In Barry P. Bosworth, Rudiger Dornbusch, Raul Laban. Eds. *The Chilean Economy: Policy Lessons and Challenges*. Washington, D.C. (Brookings Institution): 257-328.

Donahue, John. 1989. *The Privatization Process*. New York (Basic Books).

Dornbusch, Rudiger; F. Sturzenegger and Holger Wolf. 1990. Extreme Inflation: Dynamics and Stabilization. *Brookings Papers on Economic Activity* 2: 1-81.

Earnst. M.; M. Alsxeev and P. Marer. 1996. *Transforming the Core: Restructuring Industrial Enterprises in Russia and Central Europe*. Boulder (Westview Press).

EIU (Economist Intelligence Unit). 1996. Jamaica Country Report 4. London.

EIU (Economist Intelligence Unit). 1998. Jamaica, Belize, Organization of Eastern Caribbean States—Country Report. London.

Feldstein, Martin. 1974. Social Security, Induced Retirement, and Aggregate Capital Accumulation. *Journal of Political Economy* 82: 905-26.

Feldstein, Martin. 1996. The Missing Piece in Policy Analysis: Social Security Reform. *The American Economic Review. Papers and Proceedings* 86.2 (May): 1-14.

Floyd, Robert; Clive S. Gray and R.P. Short. 1984. Public Enterprise in Mixed Economies: Some Macroeconomic Aspects. Washington, D.C. (IMF).

Frenkel, Jacob A. and Assaf Razin. 1987. *Fiscal Policies and the World Economy: An Intertemporal Approach*. Cambridge, MA (MIT Press).

Galiani, S. and D. Petrocolla. 1996. The Changing Role of the Public Sector: An Ex-Post View of the Privatization Process in Argentina. *The Quarterly Review of Economics and Finance* 36.2: 131-152.

Gerchunoff, P. and G. C<novas. 1994. Las Privaticaciones en la Argentina. Impactos Micro y Macroeconómicos. *Serie Reformas de Política Pública* 21. CEPAL. United Nations.

Ghosh, Atish R.; Anne Marie Gulde and Holger Wolf. 1998. Currency Boards: The Ultimate Fix? *IMF Working Paper* WP/79/8.

Gibbon, Henry. Ed. 1997. Privatisation International Yearbook. London (Privatisation International).

Government of Brazil. 1999. Letter of Intent of the Government of Brazil. March 8, 1999. Brazilia.

Government of Indonesia. 1997. Letter of Intent of the Government of Indonesia. October 31, 1997. Jakarta.

Government of Jamaica. 1996. National Industrial Policy—A Strategic Plan for Growth and Development. Kingston.

Government of Jamaica. 1996. *National Industrial Policy—A Strategic Plan For Growth and Development*. Kingston (Jamaica Information Service).

Government of Korea, 1999. Letter of Intent of the Government of Korea. March 10, 1999. Seoul.

Government of Pakistan. 1989. Civil Servants Census. Islamabad.

Government of Pakistan. 1989. Ministry of Labor, Manpower, and Overseas Pakistanis. Report of the National Manpower Commission. Islamabad.

Government of Pakistan. 1998. Enhanced Structural Adjustment Facility Policy Framework Paper, 1998/99-2001/01. Washington, D.C. (IMF).

Government of Pakistan. Government Sponsored Corporations. Islamabad.

Government of Pakistan. Public Sector Industries Annual Report. Islamabad.

Government of Thailand, 1997. Letter of Intent of the Government of Thailand. August 14, 1997. Bangkok.

Government of Thailand. 1997.Letter of Intent of the Government of Thailand. November 25, 1997. Bangkok.

Gruber, Jonathan and David Wise. 1997. Social Security Programs and Retirement Around the World. *NBER Working Paper* 6134.

Gylfason, Thorvaldur. 1998. *Privatization, Efficiency, and Economic Growth. Institute of Economic Studies Working Paper Series* W98:09. Reykjavik (University of Iceland).

Hall, Robert and Charles Jones 1996. The Productivity of Nations. *NBER Working Paper* 5812.

Hartwing, Karl-Heinz. 1998. Der Staat als Unternehmer: Zur Rolle der öffentlichen Unternehmen in der Sozialen Marktwirschaft. In Dieter Cassel. Ed. 1998. *50 Jahre Soziale Marktwirtschaft. Ordnungstheoretische Grundlagen, Realisierungsprobleme und Zukunftsperspektiven einer wirschaftspolitischen Konzeption.* Stuttgart (Lucius & Lucius).

Hayashi, Akifumi. 1999. Fundamental Analysis of ERM Crisis. The Case of the British Pound. University at Buffalo. Buffalo, NY. Photocopy.

HBS (Harvard Business School). 1992. Telefónica de Argentina S.A. Case N9-292-039. Cambridge, MA (Harvard). Photocopy.

HBS (Harvard Business School). 1996. The 1994-95 Mexican Peso Crisis. Case 9-296-059 (revision October 2, 1996). Cambridge, MA (Harvard). Photocopy.

HBS (Harvard Business School). 1988. HBS Case 9-389-036 (revised October 1989). Cambridge, MA (Harvard). Photocopy.

Heald. David. 1989. The United Kingdom: Privatization and its Political Context. In John Vickers and Georg Yarrow. Eds. *The Politics of Privatisation in Western Europe.* London (Frank Cass): 31-48.

Hibbs, Douglas A. 1977. Political Parties and Macroeconomic Policy. *American Political Science Review* 71: 1467-1487.

Hibbs. 1987. *The American Political Economy.* Cambridge, Mass (Harvard University Press).

Holzman, Robert. 1997. Pension Reform, Financial Market Development, and Economic Growth: Preliminary Evidence from Chile. *IMF Staff Papers* 44.2: 149-178.

Hubbard, Glenn and Kenneth Judd. 1986. Liquidity Constraints, Fiscal Policy and Consumption. *Brookings Paper on Economic Activity* 1.

Hulten, Charles R. 1997. Quality Change in the CPI. *Federal Reserve Bank of St. Louis Review* May/June: 87-106.

IMF Morning Press. 1996. The Scramble to Qualify for EU Monetary Union.

IMF Morning Press. 1996.2. September 23, 1996: 2

IMF. 1995. Severance Payments. Washington, D.C. Photocopy.

IMF. 1996. Belgium Aims for 2.9 Percent Deficit Limit. Morning Press. Washington, D.C.

IMF. 1996.2. Financial Programming and Policy: The Case of Sri Lanka. Washington, D.C. (IMF Institute).

IMF. 1998.1. World Economic Outlook. The Crisis in Emerging Markets. Washington, D.C. (IMF): 17-30.

IMF. 1998.2. Jamaica—Selected Issues. Washington, D.C. (IMF).

IMF. 1999. World Economic Outlook. Part II: 40-101. Washington, D.C. (IMF).

IMF. 1999. World Economic Outlook. Database. Washington, D.C.

Köster, Kathrin. 1998. *Privatisierung von Staatsunternehmen in Japan. Entwicklung, Dynamik und Perspektiven der privatisierten Staatsbahn.* Baden-Baden (Nomos).

Kemal, A.R. 1993. Retrenchment Policies and Labour Shedding in Pakistan. International Labour Office. *Occasional Paper* 17. Geneva (ILO).

Khan, Mohsin S. and Malcolm Knight. 1988. Fund Supported Adjustment Programs and Economic Growth. *IMF Occasional Paper* 41. Washington, D.C.

Khan, Mohsin S. and Malcolm Knight. 1991. Stabilization Programs in Developing Countries. A Formal Framework. In Mohisn S. Khan; Peter J. Montiel; and Nadeem U. Haque. *Macroeconomic Models for Adjustment in Developing Countries.* Washington, D.C. (IMF): 38-85.

Kikeri, Sunita. 1998. Privatization and Labor. What Happens to Workers When Governments Divest? *World Bank Technical Paper* 396. Washington, D.C. (World Bank).

Kirkness, Christoper and John Style.1996. Pakistan—No Deviation from the Path. In Gibbon. Henry. Ed. *Privatization Yearbook.* London (Privatization International): 284-287.

Klasen, Stephan. 1994. Human Development and Women's Lives in a Restructured Bloc: Lessens from the Developing World. In Schipke, Alfred and Alan Taylor. *The Economics of Transformation. Theory and Practice in the New Market Economies.* Berlin: Springer 1994.

Klein, Lawrence. 1960. Single Equation Versus Equation System Methods of Estimation in Econometrics. *ECTRA* 28:866-871.

Klein, M. W. 1996.Timing is All: Elections and the Duration of the United States Business Cycle. *Journal of Money, Credit and Banking* 28: 83-101.

Knauss, Fritz. 1993. Privatisierung in der Bundesrepublic Deutschland 1983-1990. In Fritz Knauss. 1993. Ed. *Privatisierungs- und Beteiligungspolitik in der Bundesrepublik Deutschland.* Baden-Baden (Nomos): 121-194.

Kochhar, Kalpana; Prakash Loungani and Mark R. Stone. 1998. The East Asian Crisis: Macroeconomic Developments and Policy Lessons. *IMF Working Paper* WP/98/128. Washington, D.C.

Kotlikoff, Laurence J. 1996. Simulating the Privatization of Social Security in General Equilibrium. *NBER Working Paper* 5776. Cambridgte, Mass.

Kopies, George and Jon Craig. 1996. Transparency in Government Operations. *Occasional Paper* 158. Washington, D.C. (IMF).

Kopies, George and Steven Symansky. 1998. Fiscal Policy Rules. *Occasional Paper* 162. Washington, D.C. (IMF).

Kornai, János. 1992. *The Socialist System: The Political Economy of Communism.* Princeton (University Press).

Krugman, Paul.1994. The Myth of Asia's Miracle. *Foreign Affairs* 73.6: 62-79.

Kydland, Finn E. and Edward C. Prescott. 1982. Time to Build and Aggregate Fluctuations. *Econometrica* 50: 1345-1370.

Leibenstein, Henry. 1966. Allocative Efficiency Versus X-Efficiency. *American Economic Review* 56: 392-415.

López-de-Silanes, Florencio; Andrei Shleifer and Robert W. Vishny. 1995. Privatization in the United States. *NBER Working Paper* 5113.

Leamer, Edward W. 1983. Let's Take the Con Out of Econometrics. *American Economic Review* 73.3.

Leamer, Edward W. 1985. Sensitivity Analysis Would Help. American Economic Review 75.5.

Leibfritz, Willi, et.al. 1995. Ageing Populations, Pension Systems and Government Budgets: How do they Affect Saving? *OECD Economics Department Working Paper* 155. Paris (OECD).

Leiderman, Leonardo and Mario I. Blejer. 1988. Modelling and Testing Ricardian Equivalence. *IMF Staff Papers*.35.1.

Levine, Ross and David Renelt.1992. A Sensitivity Analysis of Cross-Country Growth Regressions. *American Economic Review* 82.4: 942-63.

Lewis-Beck, Michael S.1988. *Economics and Elections: The Major Western Democracies.* Ann Arbor (University of Michigan Press).

Liberalization and Privatization: An Overview. In El-Naggar, Said. Privatization and Structural Adjustment in Arab Countries. Washington, D.C. (IMF).

Lindgren, Carl-Johan; Gillian Garcia and Matthew I. Saal. 1996. *Bank Soundness and Macroeconomic Policy.* Washington, D.C. (IMF).

Lipton, David and Jeffrey Sachs. 1990. Privatization in Eastern Europe: The Case of Poland. *Brookings Papers on Economic Activity* 2:293-335.

Long, John B. and Charles I. Plosser. 1983. Real Business Cycles. *Journal of Political Economy* 91: 39-69.

Lucas, Robert E. 1986. Principles of Fiscal and Monetary Policy. *Journal of Monetary Economy* 17 (January): 117-134.

Lue Lim, Gail. 1991. Jamaica's Financial System: Its Historical Development. Kingston (Bank of Jamaica).

Mackensie, George A., Philip Gerson, and Alfredo Cuevas. 1997. Pension Regimes and Saving. *IMF Occasional Paper* 153. Washington, D.C. (IMF).

Mackenzie, George A. 1997. The Macroeconomic Impact of Privatization. *IMF Paper on Policy Analysis and Assessment* PPAA/97/9. Washington, D.C.

Mankiw, Gregory N. 1990. A Quick Refesher Course in Macroeconomics. *Journal of Economic Literature.* 28: 1645-1660.

Markey, Patrick. 1991. A Practitioner's Guide to Debt for Equity Swaps: The Argentine Model. *Law and Policy in International Business* 23.1: 239-261.

Masihuddin, Mohammed. 1994. Background Information on Privatization in Pakistan. Islambad (Photocopy).

Maskin, Eric S. 1992. Auctions and Privatizaiton. In Horst Siebert. Ed. *Privatization*. Tübingen (Mohr): 115-136.

McHale, John. 1995. Governance Arrangements and Transformational Slumps. Harvard University. Cambridge, Mass. Photocopy.

Megginson, William L and Jeffry M. Netter. 1998. From State to Market: A Survey of Empirical Studies on Privatization. *NYSE Working Paper* 98-05.

Megginson, William L.; Robert C. Nash and Matthias Van Randenborgh. 1994. The Financial and Operating Performance of Newly Privatized Firms: An International Empirical Analysis. *The Journal of Finance* 49.2: 403-452.

Mikkelsen, Jan G. 1998. A Model for Financial Programming. *IMF Working Paper WP/98/80*. Washington, D.C.

Ministry of Finance. 1998. Statement by Dr. The Hon. Omar Davies in the House of Representatives. Kingston. July 14, 1998. Photocopy.

Monopolkommission. 1996. Hauptgutachten. Baden-Baden.

Morgan Stanley Dean Witter Data Base. 1999. London.

Munla, Nadim. 1992. External Debt Policy. In Davis, Jeffrey. Ed. *Macroeconomic Adjustment: Policy Instruments and Issues*. Washington, D.C. (IMF Institute): 63-75.

Naqvi, Syed Nawab Haider and A.R. Kemal. 1991. The Privatization of the Public Industrial Enterprises in Pakistan.*The Pakistan Development Review* 30.2: 105-144.

Nordhaus, William. 1975. The Political Business Cycle. *Review of Economic Studies* 42: 169-190.

OECD. 1993. OECD Economic Studies 21. Paris (OECD): 7-56.

OECD. 1994. Employment Outlook. Paris (OECD).

OECD. 1994. Trends and Policies in Privatization. Paris (OECD).

OECD. 1996. Financial Market Trends 64. Paris (OECD).

Pinheiro, Armando Castelar and Ben Rorss Schneider. 1994. The Fiscal Impact of Privatization in Latin America. *The Quarterly Review of Economics and Finance* 43: 9-42.

Prébisch, Raúl. 1950. *The Economic Development of Latin America and its Principal Problems*. New York (United Nations).

Privatisation Commission. 1994. Privatization in Pakistan: Policy and Programmes. Islamabad. Photocopy.

Radelet, Steven and Jeffrey Sachs. 1998. The Onset of the East Asian Financial Crisis. Harvard Insitute for International Development. Cambridge, M.A. Photocopy.

Ranis, Gustav and Syed Akhtar Mahmood.1992. *The Political Economy of Development Policy Change*. Cambridge, MA (Basil and Blackwell).

Rodríguez, Jacobo L. 1999. Chile's Private Pension System at 18: Its Current State and Future Challenges. *Social Security and Privatization* 17: 1-23.

Roubini, Nouriel and Sala-I-Martin. 1995. A Growth Model of Inflation, Tax Evasion and Financial Repression. *Journal of Monetary Economics* 35: 275-301.

Rodrik, Dani. 1996. Understanding Economic Policy Reform. *Journal of Economic Literature* 34: 9-41.

Sachs, Jeffrey and Andrew M. Warner. 1996. Achieving Rapid Growth in the Transition Economies of Central Europe. Harvard Institute for International Development. Cambridge, Mass. Photocopy.

Sachs, Jeffrey; Aaron Tornell and Andres Velasco. 1996. Financial Crises in Emerging Markets: The Lessons from 1995. *Brookings Papers on Economic Activity* 1: 147-198.

Sala-i-Martin, Xavier 1997. I Just Ran Four Million Regressions. Washington, D.C. (Photocopy).

Salomon Smith Barney. 1998. Private Pension Funds in Latin America.—1998 Update. New York.

Sarel, Michael. 1995. Growth in East Asia: What We Can and What We Cannot Infer From It. *IMF Working Paper* WP/95/98. Washington, D.C.

Schipke, Alfred. 1994. The Political Economy of Privatization. In Alfred Schipke and Alan Taylor. Eds. *The Economics of Transformation. Theory and Practice in the New Market Economies.* Heidelberg (Springer-Verlag): 171-189.

Schulknecht, Ludger.1996. Political Business Cycles and Fiscal Policy. *Kyklos* 49: 155-170.

Schumacher, Ute and Gladstone Hutchinson (1991). Privatization in Developing Economies: The Case of Jamaica. In Ott, Attiat F. and Keith Hartley. Eds. *Privatization and Economic Efficiency. A Comparative Analysis of Developed and Developing Countries.* Brookfield, VT (Edward Elgar): 223-251.

Scully, Gerald W. 1994. The Institutional Framework and Economic Development. *Journal of Political Economy* 96.3: 652-662.

Shapiro, Carl and Robert Willig. 1990. Economic Rationales for the Scope of Privatization. In B.N. Suleiman and J. Waterbury. Eds. *The Political Economy of Public Sector Reform and Privatization.* London (Westview Press): 55-87.

Siebert, Horst. Ed. 1998. Redesigning Social Security. Tübingen (Mohr Siebeck).

Siegmund. Uwe. 1996. Are there Nationalization-Privatization Cycles? A Theoretical Survey and Empirical Results. *Kiel Institute of World Economics Working Paper* 757. Photocopy.

Solow, Robert M. 1956. A Contribution to the Theory of Economic Growth. *Quarterly Journal of Economics* 70.1: 65-94.

Stone, Carl. 1991. Putting Enterprise To Work—The Jamaican Divestment Experience. Caribbean Affairs: 12-23.

Sunday Herald, June 22, 1997. Government Bails out Ronnie Thwaites.

Swan, Trevor W. 1956. Economic Growth and Capital Accumulation. *Economic Record* 32: 327-368.

Tanzi, Vito. 1998. The Demise of the Nation State? *IMF Working Paper* WP/98/120.

The Gleaner, May 13, 1999. Coffee Board Broke.

The Gleaner, October 15, 1996

The Institute for International Finance. 1998. Capital Flows to Emerging Market Economies. January 29, 1998 quoted in Radelet and Sachs. 1998.

The Sunday Observer. 1997. Committee Calls For $-2-b Coffee Bail-out. April 6, 1997.

Tirole, Jean. 1988. The Theory of Industrial Organization. Cambridge, Mass (MIT Press).

Transel, Aysit. 1996. Workers Displaced Due to Privatization in Turkey: Before Versus After Displacement." Paper Prepared for a World Bank Conference on Public Sector Retrenchment and Efficient Compensation Schemes, November 6-7. Washington, D.C. (World Bank).

United States Department of Commerce. 1995. Jamaica—Investor Attitude Study. Washington, D.C. Photocopy.

United States Foreign Service. 1998. Country Commercial Guide Jamaica. Washington, D.C. Photcopy.

VDR (Verein Deutscher Rentenversicherungsträger). 1995. PROGNOS-Gutachten. Frankfurt. Photocopy.

Vickers, John S. and George K. Yarrow. 1988. *Privatization: An Economic Analysis*. Cambridge, MA (MIT Press).

Vuylstek. Charles. 1989. *Techniques of Privatization of State-Owned Enterprises.—Methods and Implementation*. Vol 1. Washington, D.C. (World Bank).

Waigel, Theo. 1995. Rede des Bundesministers der Finanzen anläßlich des Vorstandstreffens der Unternehmen mit (ehemaliger) Bundesbeteiligung am 14. und 15. September 1995 in Ludwigslust und Schwerin. Ministry of Finance. Photocopy.

Waternabe, Susumu. 1994. Restructuring of the Japanese National Railways: Implications for Labour. *International Labor Review* 133.1: 89-111.

Welfens, Paul J.J. 1994. Foreign Direct Investment and Privatization. In Alfred Schipke and Alan Taylor. Eds. *The Economics of Transformation. Theory and Practice in the New Marekt Economies*. Heidelberg (Springer-Verlag): 129-169.

Welfens, Paul J.J. 1996. Privatization, Efficiency and Equity. *European Institut for International Economic Relations Discussion Paper* 14. Potsdam.

West, Darrel. 1988. Gramm-Rudman-Hollings and the Politics of Debt Reduction. *Annals of the American Academy of Political Science and Social Science* 499: 90-100.

Wong, Chorng-huey and Øystein Pettersen. 1979. Financial Programming in the Framework of Optimal Control. Weltwirtschaftliches Archiv 115.1: 20-37.

World Bank. 1993. *The East Asian Miracle. Economic Growth and Public Policy*. Washington, D.C. (Oxford University Press).

World Bank. 1994. Averting the Old-Age Crisis: Policies to Protect the Old and Promote Growth. New York (Oxford University Press): 73-99.

World Bank. 1997. World Development Report. Washington, D.C. (World Bank).

World Development Report. 1995. Washington, D.C. (World Bank).

Xiao, Geng. 1991. Managerial Autonomy, Fringe Benefits, and Ownership Structure: A Comparative Study of Chinese State and Collective Enterprises. *China Economic Review* 2(1): 47-73.

Young, Alwyn. 1994. The Tyranny of Numbers: Confronting the Statistical Realities of the East Asian Growth Experience. *Quarterly Journal of Economics* 110: 641-680.

Young, Peter and Paul Reynolds. 1994. *The Amnesia of Reform* London (Adam Smith Institute).

Druck: Strauss Offsetdruck, Mörlenbach
Verarbeitung: Schäffer, Grünstadt